I0429090

INFORMATION OVERLOAD PARADOX

DROWNING IN INFORMATION, STARVING FOR KNOWLEDGE

L. V. Orman

TABLE OF CONTENTS

INTRODUCTION

THE PARADOX

Where is the wisdom we have lost in knowledge? Where is the knowledge we have lost in information? T.S. Eliot [24]

We are living in an age of information. Staggering amounts of information are collected, stored, and widely disseminated. Yet, we may be less informed and less knowledgeable than ever. The paradox of increasing information, yet decreasing knowledge and insight has many possible reasons, some of which are subtle and difficult to identify, and even more difficult to remedy. The fundamental issue is quantity crowding out quality, leading to an abundance of poor quality information which may not be a good substitute for scarce but high quality information. Information is not unique in exhibiting this paradox. There are many other goods that exhibit this unusual characteristic of more being worse than less. Those who eat the most food are rarely the healthiest people, and they may actually be severely deficient in some nutrients. Those who have the most Facebook friends are often the loneliest people. Those who are the busiest are not the most productive. Those who read books and watch television the most are sometimes the least knowledgeable. Information overload is like a raging fire, as shown in the cover of this book. There is so much heat, yet no useful heat can be extracted from it. Or it is like a raging flood. There is so much water, yet no useful water can come out of it. All of these examples point to the pervasiveness of this paradox, but it is most insidious with information, critical in an information economy, and most difficult to overcome in a modern society dominated by communication technologies. In an information economy, we appear to be shipwrecked, surrounded by an ocean of water, yet dying of thirst! The following animation demonstrates the paradox vividly. [https://media.giphy.com/media/l3V0uw1OCh2FqmUuc/giphy.gif]

Information is neutral with respect to objective and value; but knowledge is the information that is useful. As such, knowledge is specific to an objective; it is value-laden, and its quality is critically important. Yet, quantity may crowd out quality for three fundamental reasons. The most obvious is the substitution problem where the emphasis on quantity shifts the emphasis and resources away from quality. It is costly to produce quality information, and it is difficult to do both quality and quantity. When quality does not pay in proportion to its high cost, quantity wins over. This is also the most common explanation for non-information examples, but explanation for information products involves two other reasons. The second reason is the obsolescence problem. Information is not neutral with respect to the physical world, but it is an agent of change. Information is useful precisely because it is used to change the environment and subjugate nature and society to our purposes. But as information is used to change the environment to take advantage of new opportunities, our existing information about the environment becomes obsolete, leading to a loss of information. The net effect may be positive or negative, but increasingly negative as we will show, in a fast-changing information-intensive society. The third reason is the competition problem when information is used as a competitive weapon against others, to mislead and confuse others, leading to a loss of knowledge on their part. Information is power, because it can be used to control others and exploit them, by controlling their information sources, and consequently their behavior. But replacing reliable information with distorted and misleading information leads to a net information loss on their part. More importantly, if everybody uses the same tactics, leading to an information war, everybody may end up worse off with significant loss of knowledge and insight by all. We will describe all three reasons in detail in the following sections.

PART 1

SUBSTITUTION

We are buried beneath the weight of information, which is being confused with knowledge. Quantity being confused with abundance; and wealth being confused with happiness. Tom Waits [101]

Substitution of quantity for quality can take place in three different ways: by substituting cheap for expensive, complex for simple, or formal for informal. In each case, new information can actually reduce our knowledge about the world around us, if it fails to adequately replace the knowledge it substitutes. Additional information can actually reduce our total knowledge! That is the paradox! We will discuss each in the following three chapters.

CHAPTER 1

COST

We often know the price of everything, but the value of nothing!

If you believe money can't buy happiness, you probably don't know where to shop.

The modern age can be characterized by the abundance of cheap alternatives to traditionally expensive resources. Food, which has been the bane of human existence, is suddenly abundant in the Western World. Industrial farming practices produce large quantities of food, but they rely on artificial fertilizers, pesticides, and new breeds that are amenable to industrial production and long-haul transportation. The content of these new farm products is not always exactly the same as the traditional ones. The nutritional value occasionally suffers, and taste often diminishes, because the emphasis is on quantity and cost of production, not on quality. Combined with the industrial food processing that often accompanies industrial farming, the quality is often greatly diminished. The claim is that such a sacrifice in quality is a small price to pay for the abundance of food, especially with an exponentially rising human population. Food is not the only resource where cheap dominates quality. Similarly, the fundamental human need for happiness is increasingly met very cheaply, albeit at a lower quality, by artificial drugs, prescription or otherwise, instead of the traditional and expensive pursuits of family, children, and community. It is difficult for anyone to get through a day without extensive use of artificial drugs, ranging from the morning coffee to wake up to the afternoon tea to stay focused, from a beer at lunch to the evening cocktails to relax, from the wine with dinner to the late night whiskey at the neighborhood bar to feel sociable, from the aspirin for the morning headache to the soda and candy pick me up in the afternoon, from cigarettes to get through the work day to the late night marijuana to deal with the loneliness of home life, from the sleeping pill to fall asleep to the allergy medicine to stay asleep, not to mention the myriad of prescription drugs to deal with chronic problems from backaches to high blood pressure, from depression and anxiety to sexual performance. Modern human is addicted to drugs that provide happiness on the cheap, but at a lower quality. The price for such a shortcut to happiness is of course deep unhappiness in the long run, as cheap substitutes provide quick solutions but wear out quickly; and they never fully substitute for the expensive high quality and long term solutions to happiness like family, children, careers, and community.

This may be a metaphor for information in the modern age which is characterized by an abundance of cheap and poor quality information, often mistaken for knowledge and wisdom. Fundamental social, political, economic, and scientific questions are debated ad nauseam, with no conclusion in sight. Progress is claimed routinely, yet progress is always marred by doubt, and overshadowed by unexpected consequences leading to new problems. Often there is consensus that humanity made tremendous progress during the past several millennia, with an explosion of information about our physical environment, and an increasing ability to control and manipulate that environment to serve our interests; and as a result our lives are claimed to be much better than our ancestors'. Such self-serving claims are always suspect, and should be examined very carefully. Consider the printing press which started an information revolution that continues to this day. It was followed by telegraph and telephone, then movies and television, and gained increasing speed with internet and online resources. Printing press led to an explosion of information available to the masses, most importantly the Bible. That led to decades long debates about the various interpretations of the Bible, since now everybody could read the God's word for themselves, instead of relying on a church hierarchy to interpret it for them. Previously, political struggles were naked and unabashed power struggles, for everyone to see and clearly understand. When Romans fought the Huns, when Chinese fought the Mongols, when Persian fought the Greeks, there was no pretense of a religious conflict or moral cause. These were naked power struggles and perceived as such by all the participants. But printed information allowed wide-spread propaganda and information war, and encouraged a theological and supernatural context to political struggles. Suddenly, it was more difficult to see why the conflict arose, despite an enormous amount of information and debate, in fact precisely because of the enormous amount of information and debate! More importantly, it was more difficult to resolve conflicts because the real causes were hidden behind cheap justifications. When the struggle is moral and religious, endorsed and justified by abstract and supernatural powers, there is no room for compromise. Cheap and abundant information often reduces insight!

A Google search for the Israeli-Palestinian conflict will find more information on the web than one can read in a life time, and even more debate and commentary. One can find out who fired how many missiles, who killed who, who said what, who is more moral, who the victim is, and who is supporting who, in great detail. But one would be hard pressed to find any insight into win-win solutions. A simple land ownership conflict, which is typical of 19th century warfare, with many straightforward win-win solutions such as shared-land-use or non-land-based economic development, is hidden behind cheap rhetoric of religion, tradition, and personalities, where everybody ends up paralyzed by the false and cheap issues created by information abundance.

Information is costly to produce, especially quality information, but cheap to disseminate once the infrastructure has been built. Modern communication networks reduced the cost of dissemination drastically, but producing quality information remains costly. As a result, the incentive is to emphasize cheap dissemination rather than expensive production, by producing large quantities of low quality information, but disseminate it widely, with the implicit assumption that quantity is a substitute for quality. This is the explanation for the celebrity culture where some people succeed on the basis of name recognition alone, without any particular accomplishment; yet those with extraordinary accomplishments often remain obscure, poor, and unappreciated. Consider musicians. Quality music is very costly to create, and there are very few composers and song writers who produce high quality music. They often live in obscurity because high quality music rarely has mass appeal for large scale distribution; and in an era of cheap distribution, mass appeal dominates financial decisions. Mediocre music with better financial prospects then crowds out high quality music. Similar arguments apply to other information products [14].

The American poet Henry David Thoreau, upon observing the excruciatingly hard work of laying telegraph lines near his home, famously lamented: "We are in great haste to build telegraph lines from Maine to Texas, but do we have anything important enough to communicate to justify this kind of cost and effort? We are eager to tunnel under the Atlantic Ocean to bring the old world to the new, but the first news that will arrive at the American ears will probably be that Princess Adelaide has the whooping cough"! He probably would have made the same comment about the internet. With smart phones, the problem became even more acute, with a very expensive and elaborate infrastructure of wireless communication being used to transmit pictures of dancing cats and singing babies. More importantly, millions of teenagers addicted to this constant barrage of information are glued to their phones waiting for the next trivia to be texted or posted. There is an implicit assumption in diverting resources from production to dissemination that cheap dissemination is a substitute for expensive content [52]! The following cartoon demonstrates the problem vividly by portraying this new addiction, and the twisted posture it forces on people, as a Zombie Apocalypse. [https://www.facebook.com/Supercurioso/photos/a.22838556066294 0.1073741829.216841275150702/486608024840691/?type=1&theat er].

The study of history similarly suffers from a flood of cheap information overcrowding and substituting complex analysis. Every high school student knows about the assassination of the Roman emperor Julius Cesar, with all the excruciating details of his stabbing by his colleagues on the Senate floor including his protégé Brutus, and even the actual words exchanged during the stabbing. But how many know the political struggles that led to this assassination? How many high school classes actually cover the socialist tendencies of Julius Cesar, his attempts to redistribute land and free some slaves in an effort to stave off slave rebellions, and how those initiatives were resented by the wealthy land owner senators? How many college students or even the professional historians know the real political issues, instead of the cheap tawdry details? Ironically, those who know the most simplistic details often know the least about the complex real issues.

Economists have known for some time that low quality drives out high quality when it is difficult to distinguish between them, called the "lemons problem". When the marketplace cannot distinguish quality easily, the consumers tend to buy the cheaper alternative to reduce their risk, and those who produce high quality expensive products cannot compete and leave the market [22]. Information products fit well into this model, because they are notoriously difficult to distinguish in quality, since there are no obvious markers of quality information. Examples are abound. People with most Facebook friends are among the loneliest, because Facebook provides large numbers of low quality superficial friendships, but takes away time from building high quality but time consuming friendships. When it is difficult to distinguish between the two types of friendships by not understanding why one may not be a good substitute for the other, the incentives are for developing the easy friendships with minimal cost. Lemons problem extraordinaire! People who eat the most food are not the healthiest, and in fact they may have serious nutritional deficiencies. That is because they tend to eat low quality foods, since high quality foods tend to be expensive and difficult to get in large quantities, but low quality foods may not be a good source of nutrients in any quantity. Yet, when the quality is difficult to distinguish, and low quality foods look and taste similar to their high quality alternatives, the incentives are for filling up on cheap food. People who are the busiest may not be the most productive, because they fill their time with low quality insignificant activities. That is because high quality activities take planning, organization and money, and when the distinction is not obvious, the incentive is to fill one's time with the easy but insignificant activities. Those who read the most books and watch the most television are not always the best informed, because they read and watch low effort and low quality books and programs. High quality books are hard to read, and when the distinction is not obvious, the incentives are to entertain your family with the easy-to-read books and easy to watch television programs about celebrities and sports, not complex social and philosophical issues. The following cartoon shows that many superficial friends may not be a good substitute for a few high quality friends [http://jokideo.com/funny-funeral-cartoons/].

Consider academic research. Academic articles all look very similar in style and presentation, but high quality articles are much more costly to produce. If the quality is difficult to ascertain, then the likely outcome is large numbers of low quality articles, and a proliferation of low quality fields. The peer review system, although revered by the universities, does not solve this problem, because the peers of low quality producers are likely to be low quality producers themselves, and may not even recognize high quality work. More importantly, peers have no incentive to pay the high price of evaluating quality in terms of time and effort. This may explain the proliferation of new fields of study, and the increasing numbers of Ph.D.'s and academic publications, where large quantity invariably chases out high quality. The following cartoon demonstrates the challenge of the peer review system [https://www.facebook.com/ProfessorNicolaiJFoss/photos/a.50372 7862996814.1073741825.480426721993595/899823803387216/?t ype=3&theater].

Harvard economist John Kenneth Galbraith once lamented that the shifting emphasis in economic research from qualitative analysis to empirical data analysis had impoverished the field of economics. That is because the emphasis had shifted from domain knowledge and insight to learning and properly using statistical tools. The qualitative research could not compete with empirical work, not because it was lower quality, but because empirical work was more easily produced and evaluated and hence less risky. Ph.D. students could count on finishing on time, and the universities could count the number of publications by each faculty member for evaluation purposes. Qualitative work was risky, subjective to evaluate, and difficult to predict success. As a result, empirical work crowded out qualitative work, and academic evaluations were reduced to counting the number of publications per year [33].

Obsession with tools dominates many fields from literature to physics, and generates a lot of information. Modern fiction in the form of a novel often devotes many pages to character development, in addition to the substance of the novel. Character development is an arduous task to write, and even to read. Often the main message is lost in the detail of character development, or there is no specific message, but just beautiful prose. Poetry is a similar obsession with very strict rules as tools, and the message is often obscured by the structure, and left open to interpretation. That emphasis on structure often allows the writer to write a great deal and beautifully, without saying anything specific, or saying rather simple things in rather elaborate and convoluted ways, just to impress the reader with complexity and the intricacy of the tool and the effort required to compose it and to read it. Statistics is another formal tool that generates enormous amount of information, both the quantity of data collected, and also the number of conclusions reached. Data collected is not always relevant to the task, and the conclusions reached are not always right. But that only encourages more debate and more discussion, and the tentativeness of the conclusions is revered as the scientific process. The emphasis appears to be on establishing a well-defined set of tools and processes, rather than on quickly discovering truth and easily discarding falsehoods. Discovering lots of half-truths tentatively and publicizing them appear to be preferable to limiting findings and public announcements to water-tight reliable conclusions. Medical research may be a prime example. Half-truths and plausible conjectures are constantly propagated as new and revolutionary treatments that get attention and build careers, always with the caveat that the findings are tentative and require much more careful analysis. Such excessive publicity around merely plausible conjectures exaggerates scientific progress, and creates a false sense of knowledge and overconfidence, and eventually erodes the public confidence in scientific findings. The anti-science movement in the US is a direct result of such unjustified hype and exaggeration of scientific findings, especially in biological and social sciences, but also increasingly in physical sciences.

Similarly, UCLA statistician Judea Pearl criticizes social science research as overly concerned with statistical tools, and not enough with insight and policy recommendations. In fact, he argued that the emphasis on statistical tools made social science research less relevant to understanding and solving real social problems. In every empirical research paper he colorfully pronounced that there is one section that is completely nonscientific: it is always titled conclusions, and that is where the authors often draw policy implications. But policy implications require an understanding of causality so that one can manipulate causes to change effects. Yet, statistical data analysis without experiments rarely provides insight into causality, but only correlation, and the policy conclusions drawn are merely opinions with little scientific basis. That is why most every research paper ends with an urgent plea to do more research to justify the conclusions, and almost never ends a debate conclusively. Moreover, one can potentially find some statistical evidence to support any hypothesis, because 95% significance test is rather weak when so many researchers are repeating the same tests again and again with different data sets, and ignoring the failures, and publishing the rare successes. The inability to replicate most research findings is a troubling consequence of this research environment. As a result, the explosion of research activity does not provide better insight into any of the hypotheses tested. This is how quantity overcrowds quality even in scientific research [77].

Consider a highly publicized research article by Cornell psychologist Daryl Bem in which he found statistically significant evidence that humans can predict purely random future events [10]. Such clairvoyance contradicts the laws of physics as we know them. Consequently, this research presents a dilemma to either reject the laws of physics governing time and randomness, or reject the rules of statistical significance. Either option requires invalidating a large amount of existing human knowledge. There is evidence that either choice is possible. The laws of physics may be different at very small and very large scales than the ones that operate at human scale so human neurobiology may not be governed by the familiar rules of physics; or the statistical significance tests may be too weak rendering most knowledge in social sciences unreliable. Weak statistical tests may be producing large quantities of highly unreliable information both in sciences and social sciences, substituting cheap hypotheses for expensive and reliable conclusions. A major social science journal recently announced that 95% statistical significance test, that has been the mainstay of social science research, would no more be sufficient for academic publication of research articles, lending support to this argument [70].

Psychologists are not the only ones struggling with the abundance of cheap low quality information. Neuroscience is another good example. Functional MRI images of the brain revolutionized neuroscience where researchers can easily image the brain in real time as it is involved in a task, and determine which parts of the brain are active by observing the blood flow. But the methodology is not reliable, and as cheap as it is, it also produces a great deal of false positives. When you divide the brain into thousands of small regions, and make millions of observations trying to find statistically significant patterns, there are huge risks of error, especially when the bulk of the work is done by black box software which is itself poorly understood. In 2009, a graduate student in University of California at Davis set out to show that the results from functional MRI were mostly nonsensical noise. He conducted an experiment involving a dead salmon. He showed the dead salmon pictures of humans, while scanning his brain, and found significant brain activity in different regions of the brain suggesting that the salmon was responding to human pictures, and trying to identify them s unique individuals. Remember it was a salmon, and it was dead!

This problem is not limited to neuroscience. In practically every field of science and social science, researchers are using sophisticated software products that they have little understanding, especially of its limitations. Machine Learning is the newest field in statistics that provides black box tools to be used in fields ranging from physics to psychology, but the researchers have no understanding of how and why it works, and under what conditions. And just because it happens to work well for some problems under some conditions is no guarantee that it will work for different problems under different conditions. This is a recipe for producing large quantities of low quality and unreliable information masquerading as useful knowledge [117].

Consider the markets versus government debate, which is the fundamental economic policy question of our time. The debate focuses on which one is more efficient in allocating resources, when in fact the critical question is who benefits from these institutions, since they are controlled by different constituencies, but that question is rarely asked. Either institution can be quite efficient if well designed, but in real life they are both quite inefficient because of manipulation by opposing political forces, so asking for political beneficiaries of these institutions is critical. Markets are prone to manipulation by the economically powerful, and the governments are prone to political interference by powerful organized interest groups. Markets are rarely efficient, although economists like to talk about efficient markets; because no business likes to be in a head-to-head competition with other businesses, as the economists advocate; so they try to gain market power by acquiring their competitors, by colluding with them, or by destroying them through competitive action. Governments are rarely efficient because bureaucracies have their own narrow interests, and they expand to promote those interests at the expense of their constituencies. Moreover, the analyses of efficiency are never complete because they routinely ignore the cost of achieving that efficiency. In case of markets, that is the cost of market making, including the costs of running banks, stock exchanges, and advertising campaigns, and their highly paid professionals. In case of governments, that is the cost of the bureaucracy, and the cost of influencing and informing the bureaucracy through lobbyists and special interest lawyers. The fundamental issue is how to design good markets and good governments. The solution to market inefficiencies is not necessarily more government, and the solution to government inefficiency is not necessarily more markets, although the question is often posed in that fashion. Moreover, markets and governments interact in complex ways, making good design even more critical. Markets need governments and vice versa. What would the auto industry be like without the government built infrastructure of highways and bridges? How would private banks operate without government imposed currency and law enforcement with national and international reach? Can governments operate without some degree of decentralization, and market-like competition among the governments of different types and different levels? How much centralization and how many levels of government is optimum with what granularity? These are the hard and high quality questions that are not asked. Instead, the simple markets versus government debate generates a lot of low quality information, because they are easier to debate and get an audience, in a clear case of quantity chasing out quality [33]. Meanwhile all bureaucracies are terribly inefficient with endless meetings to negotiate turf battles among their own ranks, with less concern for serving their constituents. The following cartoon nicely depicts the inefficiency of organizational life dominated by group meetings.

[https://www.facebook.com/Tutor2u/photos/a.654066544639817.107 3741828.128272983885845/909117605801375/?type=3&theater]

There is an explosion of information about financial markets. Not a minute goes by without some national news channel on television, radio, or the web, reporting on the stock prices, exchange rates, or bond yields. The combination of disclosure laws and modern information technology allows us to know more than ever about the financial markets ranging from the latest SEC filings by each firm, the expectations of market analysts for each firm, and the latest bit of gossip or rumor posted on financial blogs. Yet we may know less about the financial markets than ever. We may have more cheap financial data at our fingertips, but the amount of hidden expensive financial information grew even more, leaving the public relatively more ignorant. That is the paradox. More information in public view does not make us more knowledgeable, when the information hidden from public view grows even larger and more consequential. The private equity industry, which takes companies private, outside the view of SEC and the public filings, more than tripled in size in 2000's. Over the counter derivatives, which are traded one-to-one away from the prying eyes of the main stock exchanges almost doubled during the same decade. It was a part of this market, credit default swaps, which led to the financial crisis of 2008. Because credit default swaps were not traded on a public exchange, no one knew what anyone else's outstanding liability was, and what their risk of insolvency was. Yet, despite the financial crisis that resulted from this ignorance, the market for over-the-counter derivatives continues to grow by leaps and bounds. Add to this, a shadow banking system that operates outside the existing banking regulatory regime, and hence largely hidden from view. A 2010 report by the New York Federal Reserve Bank found that the shadow banking system was almost twice as large as the regulated and visible banking system. So, we find ourselves in a paradoxical situation of knowing too much, yet not enough! We know the latest gossip about celebrities, but not the extent of our drone warfare; we have access to every single page of the two thousand-page Patient Protection and Affordable Care Act of the Obama Administration, yet we do not know what promises were made to large pharmaceutical companies to get it passed; we have access to all major newspapers of the world on the web, yet we do not know which major financial institutions might be insolvent. We know too much of the cheap and trivial information, but not enough of the expensive and consequential information [112]

Consider the issue of meritocracy versus aristocracy. The American ideal is a purely meritocratic society where anybody can succeed if they work hard enough, with no aristocratic class that inherits privileges. The debates about the democratic value of meritocracy, and the unfairness of aristocracy rage on. But meritocracy is an illusion. Nobody wants to be in a head-to-head competition with everybody else in a purely meritocratic society. Anybody who succeeds on the basis of pure merit has all the incentives to pull the ladder behind them and make it difficult for the others to succeed. And that is exactly what happens. There is very little difference between aristocracies and meritocracies since both lead to a small group of elites controlling a large portion of resources. In either system, those who make it to the top always try hard to stay there without being challenged. They do it by excluding the riffraff from their country clubs, elite universities, corporate advisory boards, private schools, social networks, and of course from their inheritance. The children of the elite are never failures. Billionaire Warren Buffet famously announced that his wealth would go to charity rather than his children, but children also inherit the social network of their parents, and that is probably more valuable than the billions they could inherit, and they are all already wealthy in their own right. Meritocracies, just like aristocracies, also tend to keep their lineage in power by marrying within their class. The increasing prosperity enjoyed by professional and managerial classes is further enhanced by the recently emerging mating patterns known as assortative mating which is the tendency of people to marry their financial equivalents. Doctors used to marry nurses, and lawyers and managers their secretaries. Now elites marry within their class, which are their business or professional associates with their own lucrative careers. A 100K lawyer marries another 100K dollar lawyer; and a 20K clerk marries another 20K clerk, leading to an income differential of 200K versus 40K. Is it no wonder then that the professional class loves feminism? It allows them to maintain their class privileges or even enhance them further. The same issue underlies education. The elite university system allows the elites to consolidate their privileges. Despite all the rhetoric about the equalizing effect of education, scholarships for the poor, and ethnic and racial diversity, universities remain elite institutions. Their student bodies come overwhelmingly from privileged backgrounds, because the admittance requirements are strict and require an elite background either academically, or in social or athletic engagement. Those with privileged backgrounds ranging from private tutors to successful role models, from a healthy diet to stimulating extra-curricular activities, from inherited intelligence and physical beauty to an inherited superior ability to manipulate abstract symbols and concepts as opposed to underappreciated ability to work with your hands, all allow the maintenance of elite privileges over generations. The occasional break into elite institutions by lower classes actually make matters worse, by taking away the potential leaders of lower classes and converting them into elites, which leaves lower classes without adequate leadership in defending their class interests. There is nothing more effective in breaking down class consciousness and class struggle than taking their most able leaders and converting them to elites. Meritocracy does exactly that! More importantly, it creates the illusion of wide spread social mobility and a democratization of access to privileges, which allows elites to be even more self-aggrandizing and self-righteous, and dismissive of the lower class struggles. They feel even more entitled to their privileges as they view themselves as self-made successes, and more disdainful of the lower classes and their needs, since presumably they all had equal opportunity and a fair chance to compete, and simply failed to measure up! Democratic equalizing value of meritocracy is an illusion. Yet, the debates comparing aristocracies and meritocracies are cheap and easy to understand, and they dominate the discussions, instead of social mobility and wealth inequality. The critical complex issue that needs to be discussed is the outcome of social mobility from one class to another, not the vague ideological arguments that make no practical difference [112, 113, 116].

Similarly, ethnic and religious differences as an explanation of political conflict and warfare are common, and generate a lot of information and debate. Yet, they only obscure the real political and economic reasons for conflict and warfare. Religion and ethnicity are easy to understand and debate, yet they are low quality information, because they are often the superficial reason for conflict. They are merely the organizing principle for the parties to wage war effectively, not the underlying cause of the conflict. Nation-states serve the same purpose of organizing large groups to wage war effectively, but nation-states are not the cause of conflict. It is often surprising to hear a resource based analysis of current conflicts, such as the access to water resources fueling the conflict in Syria, and the distribution of oil revenues creating the conflict in Iraq. It is much easier to talk about ethnic and religious rivalries, which give no insight into possible compromise solutions. After all, a religious conflict does not lend itself to a compromise [6]! The following news video is typical of how religious conflict is reported as trivial quarrels, instead of long standing fundamental conflicts of interest [https://www.facebook.com/100004978396212/videos/517432198432722/?pnref=story].

Conflict resolution becomes difficult when the real causes of conflict are obfuscated by simplistic debates. In every military conflict around the world, the US government poses two questions: Should we intervene, and if yes, on which side". Those are precisely the wrong questions to ask, although they are cheap to ask. After all, those are not the questions we ask when we face domestic conflict. When the police arrive at a crime scene, they do not ask: "should we intervene, and if yes, on which side"! They always intervene, and always remain neutral. Similarly, in a connected world, all conflicts have a tendency to spread, and all conflicts have effects far and wide. We always need to intervene, and never on one side, but take a neutral position as much as possible, and try to find compromise solutions. Imagine if the US had taken such positions in the Palestinian, Iraqi, Syrian, and Afghan conflicts. Of course a neutral intervention does not have to be timid. It could be very aggressive diplomatically, and even militarily, but it aims to resolve the conflict, rather than bolster one side towards an unconditional victory. Such intervention would be much more effective when it is taken by a large alliance of nations, and building such an international infrastructure of alliances would be the ground work that would make conflict resolution more effective. After all, United Nations was an attempt at precisely that objective. But it is just a first step. A complex international legal system would also be necessary, including universal rights for all world citizens, groups, and institutions that override national laws, and a process to intervene quickly, effectively, and internationally in all conflicts to protect those rights when they come into conflict with national laws. Standard procedures have to be developed to create incentives for all parties to cooperate or face wide spread international economic and military punishment, and financial resources have to be available to be deployed quickly into conflict areas to remedy economic grievances, and also to create further incentives for all to cooperate. Without such complexity, United Nations becomes a simple debating platform which adds to the information overload, without accomplishing anything concrete.

Political activism and protest movements similarly suffer from a great deal of cheap information and analysis that obscures the real grievances. The protesters are often simply angry about their lives, and direct that anger randomly towards any cause that appears to provide some relief, with no real understanding of the political causes they are supporting. The placards they carry, and the slogans they chant are often simple and devoid of any meaning as demonstrated in the following cartoon

[https://www.facebook.com/photo.php?fbid=1127600993923052&set =a.600220263327797.147731.100000194859039&type=1&theater].

A more meaningful set of placards might contain complaints like "How come nobody loves me?", "Why don't I have a high paying job?", or "Why don't I have any friends?" Those would be the real concrete issues that motivate people and could be resolved only if they were not hidden beyond cheap slogans that serve other people's interests!

German mathematician Braess showed some years ago that more and cheaper information may leave   everybody worse off. He called it Braess' Paradox. This happens because cheap information may have hidden costs that are born by others, and when everybody goes after the cheap information, and passes the costs to others, everybody suffers. The original paradox involves a highway example, but it is easily extendable to information. A new efficient highway is built to provide a shortcut to a popular destination. Everybody rushes to use the shortcut to cut their commute time, and gain an advantage over others. As a result the new road gets congested very quickly, and the competitive advantage is lost, and it might even be worse than the old commute time. The paradox is that the commuters cannot leave the new road and go back to their old routes and may all end up worse off because of this new efficient shortcut. The reason for this dilemma is the adjustment everybody makes to this new route which may not be easily reversible, such as moving to the suburbs, buying a new home, the city eliminating the bus service, and the connecting roads being congested which may be critical to all the alternative routes. There is actually considerable evidence from urban planning that whenever a city builds a highway to the suburbs, the commute times get worse in the long run, after a short period of improvement; and the reason is of course the adjustment by the people by moving to the suburbs in large numbers, and the developers building new communities at the edges of the city to take advantage of the new highway [21].

The paradox easily extends to cheap information. Email made it very cheap to send commercial advertisements to large numbers of people. Everybody rushed in to take advantage of this new medium for commercial purposes. But before long, email accounts were flooded with unwanted commercial messages, and email became unusable, and the value of sending commercial messages dropped. But it is difficult to get out of that model, because businesses adjusted to it, and created complete departments to take advantage of cheap email advertising. More importantly, as consumers developed defenses, learned to ignore commercial messages, or installed filters to detect and eliminate them, the businesses built their own tools to bypass the filters and to forcefully catch the attention of the consumers. Such information warfare often leaves everyone worse off, but once committed to the use of email, neither the consumers nor the businesses could walk away from this new tool that provided cheap information.

This warfare is in full bloom now on the internet with ad blockers. Ad blockers are software you install to block ads on web sites, and they are an existential threat to business on the internet, since most web sites depend on ad revenue for their income, most notably giants like Google and Facebook. But as consumers install ad blockers, businesses try to find ways to bypass them, and an information war ensues, possibly leaving everyone worse off. In fact, it has been reported that the companies that make ad blocking software are also making tools to bypass them, and hence selling tools to both sides of the information war [64]. This model of course was very common in the weapons industry with big industrial states selling weapons often to both sides of any conflict in the undeveloped world, and it was always a very lucrative business. Weapons industry provides another example of cheap weapons leaving all parties worse off. Cheaper and more effective weapons give a tremendous competitive advantage to warring states, so they all rush to acquire them, as in anti-personnel mines, napalm, chemical, biological, and nuclear weapons, or drone based missiles. But as all parties acquire them, the competitive advantage is quickly lost, and all parties incur severe losses both in personnel and in money, but nobody can back away from the weapons for fear of losing even more of the competitive advantage. This is why new weapons spread very quickly, and almost always leave everyone worse off.

In the information wars, this problem is likely to get worse with the advent of big data. As sensor technology develops and starts collecting data in real time from all physical and biological processes, such as factories, farms, roadways, lakes, rivers, forests, and even from inside the human body, that data will provide a competitive advantage to those who can use it to their advantage. Imagine insurance companies having access to all the sensors collecting data about your driving practices and also your health information in real time. The consumers on the other hand will have an incentive to acquire tools to block access to such information. The following information war is likely to leave everyone worse off. Imagine a retailer who collects data about your shopping behavior, the web sites you visit, the prices you observe, and even your physical location inside their store or outside in the neighborhood, and it uses all of this information to manipulate you into buying things you don't need, or convince you to pay more than you would otherwise. Information is a powerful tool. But then, in response, you would collect information about the retailer, its price discounts, its competitors' prices, coupons it gives out, and the sales promotions it runs to reverse the information advantage it has over you? Now you both have huge amounts of information about each other that you use against each other. Is anyone better off? Are you all better informed or are you in an arms race of information that leaves everyone worse off with huge transaction costs in terms of the effort and money spent on buying and selling?

CHAPTER 2

COMPLEXITY

If there is beauty in simplicity, then modern life is quite ugly.

We frequently confuse truth with an obsessive and unnecessary dedication to accuracy and precision.

Simple questions are often expanded into complex issues and debated ad nauseam with no resolution, because complexity creates an aura of respectability and exclusiveness. It also creates experts, specialists, political activists, fund raisers, and professional debaters who build lucrative careers out of artificially created complexity.

The story goes like this. An American businessman was on vacation in a little coastal village in Mexico, and saw a fisherman coming back from the sea early in the day with only a few fish. He asks the fisherman why he didn't fish longer and catch more. The fisherman replies that he catches just enough to feed his family, and he spends the rest of the day just sitting on the beach and playing his guitar. The businessman suggests that by catching a few extra fish every day, he can generate some revenue, buy a bigger boat, start a business, and eventually even start his own processing plant, and make a lot of money. "Then what" the fisherman asks. "Then you can retire in 20 years, buy a beach house and spend the day sitting at the beach playing your guitar", the businessman says. "But I do that already" fisherman responds greatly perplexed.

We create huge amounts of information with the expectation that it will improve our lives. In fact, it rarely does. The benefits from additional information often barely pays for the additional complexity generated, with no additional benefit. Why do we do it then? Because it pays very handsomely for those creating complexity, because they can pass the costs on to others! The fisherman in the story may not benefit from the additional complexity of starting a fishing business, but the businessman certainly will, by advising him and running the business for him. More importantly, if the fisherman doesn't do it, the businessman will start the business, create additional complexity which will lead to short term advantage, and push the individual fisherman out of work. In fact, the high-tech fishing and farming industries did precisely that, and by efficiently serving complex global markets, they made subsistence fishing and farming impossible. The reason is simple. The fisherman cannot live by fish alone. He has to buy some things from others. When everybody does subsistence fishing and farming, the model works perfectly. But when some start large businesses and gain great short-term cost advantage, they increase their purchasing power, and make it impossible for the subsistence fisherman to buy anything. Add to that the elimination of fish supplies in an overfished ocean, and you have all the ingredients of a disaster for our happy subsistence fisherman. As beautiful as the story is, that lifestyle is sustainable only if everybody does it. When some don't, nobody can; and the complexity increases interminably, even if it leaves everybody worse off in the long run! That is the paradox of complexity.

Examples are abound! The benefits of college education barely pays the cost! The benefits of medical research are often less than the cost of the research facilities. The benefits from global marketplaces are often less than the cost of huge corporate bureaucracies running them. The benefits from non-profit fund- raising is often barely enough to pay the cost of fund raising. But the efforts continue to increase, because those who benefit from additional complexity are different from those who pay the cost. And those who receive the benefits push for increasing complexity as long as they are able to pass the costs on to others.

Even our entertainment is incredibly complex when it is not even clear why entertainment is needed, let alone dominate our lives. When people are asked what is most critical to their happiness; music, movies, video games, and television are always in the top ten. Some people spend their whole days plugged into their iPod or mp3 player, and their evenings connected to Netflix, Xbox, or their favorite television programs. How could such complex artificial constructs be so dominant in our lives? After all, they are mere imitations of life, not real life experiences. Entertainment is addictive, simply because it overloads our senses in a narrow area without totally replacing a simple natural experience. It is a fake experience! That overload gives a great sense of quick pleasure, yet since it is not a complete life experience, it leaves us needing more. That short term quick fix, with a need for a more complete experience is a recipe for addiction. Once addicted, we search more and more of the same fake experience, with increasing complexity, not realizing the more complex the experience, the more artificial it is, and can never substitute for a simple natural real-life experience. Such a vicious cycle creates a complex and artificial entertainment world of music, movies, and games that increasingly defines our reality, instead of the simplicity of the real-world.

This should not be surprising since we live in a largely artificial world, largely disconnected from the natural world. We live in heated and air conditioned homes, drive everywhere, and sit in an office in front of computers all day for work. Some people can go for days without ever experiencing the outside world, and months without experiencing the wild nature. Such complexity is not necessary, except that it is unavoidable in a competitive world, because it gives a short term advantage to those who embrace it. You don't have to drive a car, but you can't afford not to, when everybody else does, and gains a huge advantage of mobility over you. The long run costs to your health, or to the environment might be unacceptably high, but that doesn't change the short-run incentives. The following snippet captures the artificiality of modern life very succinctly [https://www.facebook.com/HotMomsClub/photos/a.297149881703. 141887.56843501703/10152851007041704/?type=1&theater]. The following video captures humorously the attraction of unnecessary complexity as a status symbol. https://www.facebook.com/196740567116359/videos/34419008570 4739/?pnref=story .

Moral philosophers are among the biggest contributors to unnecessary complexity. A classic ethical dilemma involves a runaway train approaching a switch. On one side of the switch there are three people standing on the tracks; on the other side there is one person standing on the tracks. You control the switch, and the train is going to kill the three on the tracks if you take no action. Would you throw the switch to kill one person instead of three? Most people say yes to minimize the number killed. Then, the question is reformulated to require you to physically throw one person under the train, to stop the train and save the three on the tracks. Most people say no to that proposition. Philosophers muse at the inconsistency and come up with complex explanations for it, since the ethical problem appears to be the same in both cases. In fact, it isn't! First of all, this is a narrow and technology dependent question. Without a train technology, or a similar technology that enables such killing, the ethical dilemma would disappear. Second, since the subject does not know any of the people on the tracks, their value to the society, their interest in life, or any other facts about them, the subject is probably indifferent between the two options. It really doesn't matter to him. The questioner is prompting the response by suggesting that killing fewer people may be more desirable. Third, from a purely personal interest perspective the two options are not equivalent. Throwing somebody under the train involves considerable effort and risk to the subject. There is a real possibility that the person may fight back to save his life! Fourth, the obvious solution is in the technology itself. Most modern trains have break systems that would alleviate this ethical problem. The important point is that most ethical questions are contrived to appear complex and universal, but in fact have rather simple and case-specific explanations and lend themselves to obvious and narrowly tailored solutions. They are neither universal nor intrinsic to the human condition. As such they require no complex universal explanations. The following cartoon captures the criticism of unnecessarily and artificially convoluted debates among moral philosophers [http://existentialcomics.com/comic/106].

We attribute complex design properties and purposeful attributes to nature, but nature is actually quite simple, and life is often short, brutish, and messy. Most life ends very quickly, even before it starts. Those who survive do it by exploiting other life forms, and have the illusion of a beautiful and complex equilibrium, simply because they survived. In fact, that equilibrium is frequently disrupted with great ferocity and destruction, and nature starts all over. In the long run, we know that most everything we know as nature will disappear and be replaced by other natures, as the universe is a dynamic place at multiple levels. Our own planet will not survive forever as the sun expands and devours it in several billion years. Few species of life would survive a catastrophic change in the environment or a significant cosmic accident. Rise of animals for example must have been an enormous shock to plants that had dominated the Earth for millions of years before then. But their very success in dominating the earth must have created the environment for new species that used abundant plants as food. Our own success also creates opportunities for other species to rise and take advantage of the environment we created. As much as we admire it, the balance and stability in nature is an illusion. We confuse interconnectedness with balance and stability. In fact, nature is a myopic hacker that constantly patches up problems with proximate solutions, with no long term vision or planning. It is always fighting fires, and never planning for the future disasters. No good planner or engineer would ever work like that! They love complexity.

Biologist Richard Dawkins has a wonderful example of the myopia in nature, and how nature often just hacks its way to quick and dirty solutions with no attention to long term consequences. Laryngeal nerve connects the brain to the larynx and activates the voice cords in throat. In humans, this nerve starts at the brain and goes all the way down to the chest, loops around the heart, and then comes back to the larynx. Obviously, a very inefficient design, compared to a direct connection which would be only a few inches. In a giraffe, with a long neck, the design looks downright silly, as it goes down six feet, the whole length of the neck, loops around the heart, and then comes back again! No engineer would make such a silly design mistake! Why would nature? It turns out in fish, where the nerve first evolved, that is the shortest route between the brain and the throat, as fish do not have necks. As other animals evolved, they adopted the most obvious and quickest solution, which is just to elongate the nerve, as they developed necks. Eventually, this quick and dirty hacking solution ended up as a rather silly design in humans and giraffes. Nature is rather simple minded. We create complexity when we try to design from scratch what nature discovered by simple trial and error and incremental change [19]. The following video demonstrates this vividly by dissecting the laryngeal nerve of a giraffe [https://www.youtube.com/watch?v=cO1a1Ek-HD0].

Education is a great example of quantity chasing out quality through unnecessary complexity. Typical American now goes through 15 years of education before being eligible for a reasonable full time job, be a productive member of the society, be financially independent, and possibly start a family of their own. The content of that education is also increasingly complex and symbolic, rather than intuitive and practical. There is a real cost to education, both in terms of providing it, paying for it, but also in terms of the delay in young people's ability to start independent adult lives. Delays in independence are costly. Teenagers are increasingly treated as children, although only a hundred years ago they were universally treated as adults with adult rights and responsibilities. Of course teenagers are not children, neither physically nor psychologically, and any effort to treat them as children leads to resentment and rebellion that is typical of adult-teen relationships in the modern world. So much so that many psychologists made careers out of explaining teenage rebellion as normal, and advising parents how to best deal with it. In fact, teenage rebellion was not a common occurrence in traditional societies, as teenagers were treated as independent adults with jobs, responsibilities, and family lives of their own. Delaying independence well beyond teens is unnatural, painful, and difficult to manage. But that is the price we pay for increased complexity of the modern world, and extended education that it requires. How much complexity is optimum when the resulting educational requirements are so costly to the society? The costs are often hidden, but very real. A life time of education, and never being ready to fully participate as an independent adult, would clearly be an anathema; yet complexity continues to increase, and professional careers require increasing amounts of education well past teenage years and into 20's. Academic careers may not even start until 30's. The costs to the individuals and the society are enormous, but they are never considered fully. Age-old simple rules about raising children, educating them, and preparing them for adulthood, are increasingly obsolete; yet the new knowledge of parenthood, as complex as it is, is not adequate for the task of managing such an extended childhood well into the 20's [15].

Delaying sexuality well beyond puberty is similarly unnatural, painful, and difficult to manage. The county of India for example, is going through a major crisis of sexual mores as it transforms from a traditional society to western culture. The primary influence of the western culture is the long years of education and the delay of adulthood, when in a traditional society people got married and started families in their teens. In a culture where sexuality is tied to marriage, extended education and the delay of marriage necessarily implies a delay of sexuality. This is where the two cultures come into serious conflict. On the one hand educational requirement delays marriage, on the other hand sex outside of the marriage is shunned. As a result, sexuality of young people is delayed well beyond puberty. Its consequences are wide-spread sexual frustration, anger, and hostility between genders, as sexual frustration builds, and often blows up into violence. It is very difficult for political leaders to identify the real causes of such crises, and to come up with comprehensive solutions, as they develop slowly over long periods of time; yet it is very easy to blame those who rebel against the rules and try to solve their own individual predicaments at the expense of others. The result is culture wars, as those committed to different cultures blame each other; or gender wars as men and women blame each other for not making the sacrifices necessary to solve the problems. Any drastic social change leads to a great deal of political struggle, as different groups try to take advantage of the crisis at the expense of others, especially because the underlying causes are difficult to identify and treat. Asking others to make sacrifices is easy and also politically beneficial. What we have in India is women blaming men for being sexually aggressive and violent, and men blaming women for being too sexual and provocative; yet the real causes of the crisis as the unresolved conflict between two cultures, in a country in transition, is widely overlooked.

At the other end of the spectrum, Scandinavian countries are increasingly abandoning the concept of protecting children from sex, and embracing sex as natural and normal to learn about at any age. Scandinavian children's books are quite sexually explicit to the extent that in a conservative country like the US they would be considered pornographic. Accompanying that kind of upbringing, there is a sexual liberation that comes with teenage years, where sexual activity is not only tolerated by encouraged. That is a sharp contrast to the US and Southern Europe where parents try their hardest to delay their children's sexuality as long as possible. The fact that Scandinavian children develop quite healthy attitudes towards sex should give pause to the other cultures, where sexual dysfunction and sex related crimes is quite common [84].

Education is changing. Online education is starting to challenge the monopoly of universities, their high cost, and their operations, but not the content of education or the length of it. There seems to be a near-consensus that more education is always better, and increasingly essential for a high-tech society, irrespective of the content of that education. The dominance of quantity over quality is most prominent when an instructor asks you to write a 30-page paper on a subject of your choosing! When the criteria for evaluation is the length of the paper and not the content or even the quality, it is obvious where the emphasis is! More importantly, most of our education is not about skills necessary for a high-tech complex society, but increasingly about intellectual debates over social and philosophical issues. Such debates dominate the liberal arts education, and they are justified as building skills of critical thinking, as opposed to disseminating known and undisputed facts and skills for jobs. These debates generate a lot of information, yet provide no obvious solutions, or even methodologies to arrive at solutions, so their quality is suspect. Every student is expected to think for themselves and reach their own conclusions. The education merely gives you some frameworks to clarify and classify the problems and possibly make some cogent arguments, with no obvious resolution of the issues. Education has become like the following calculator: not particularly useful to anyone, but it is cute and interesting[https://www.facebook.com/video.php?v=66006835079425 9&fref=nf]. Or it became like a football game: grueling for the players, fun for the observers and employers, income for the managers and bureaucracies, and easily scorable for competition.

Even more ominous is the difficulty of learning from debates. There is considerable evidence that the general public does not benefit from intellectual debates, and they can't even distinguish between profound arguments, and nonsensical arguments designed to sound like profound arguments. Debates among experts are difficult to follow because of jargon and the complexity of the arguments, so the audience is more likely to judge the credibility of the debaters rather than the strength of arguments. Because of that, the debaters tend to emphasize flashy credibility enhancing arguments, and attacks on the credibility of the others, instead of making cogent and relevant arguments. As a result, the debates lead to significantly less understanding of the real issues. In one famous experiment, the researchers asked the subjects to rate the relevance and significance of a number of arguments. Some were profound statement by serious scientists and philosophers; others were nonsensical statement randomly generated by a computer but designed to sound profound. The subjects rated them as equally profound, and could not distinguish computer generated nonsense from the real arguments [114]. Here is an example of a fake computer generated wisdom that impressed the subjects of all ages and education levels [https://www.washingtonpost.com/news/wonk/wp/2015/12/01/the-kinds-of-people-who-confuse-total-nonsense-for-something-really-deep].

One such loud and aggressive debate is between science and religion about the origins of the universe. In fact, neither science nor religion has anything useful to say about the origins of the universe, and ironically that only encourages more debate and generates a large quantity of information. Scientific discovery of the Big Bang Theory and the theory of expanding universe, as interesting as they are, say nothing about the origins of the universe, unless one can take an arbitrary moment in the history of the universe and call it the beginning. The Big Bang Theory requires the existence of mass before it, and the existence of anything before the beginning suggests that it is not the beginning. Religions suffer from the same logical folly. They explain the universe in terms of a creator, but the existence of a creator before the beginning suggests that it was not the beginning, but an arbitrary moment in its history. In fact, the concept of a "beginning" is not explainable using our existing human constructs, yet the amount of information generated from debates between alternative theories fill our libraries and school curricula. A debate between alternative theories often obscures the shortcomings common to all the proposed alternatives, but emphasizes the information that distinguishes between those theories. Shortcomings that are common to all are often much more useful to understanding, yet they are driven out by the quantity of information produced by the debate in the name of critical thinking [91]. The following cartoon humorously demonstrates the folly of such scientific debates [https://www.facebook.com/PuebloGrandeMuseum/photos/a.1537415 91308608.31043.115484175134350/1220288784653878/?type=3&the ater]

Similar debates dominate the theories explaining the beginning of life where life is defined as self-replicating organisms. Science and religion are once again adversaries, and neither has a satisfactory explanation. Scientific theory of evolution says nothing about the beginning of life, since evolution requires the existence of self-replicating organisms, and as such cannot explain how they came into existence. There are attempts to explain the beginning of life in terms of accidental chemical reactions. But that explanation relies on intrinsic characteristics of the elements comprising the earth, but since we don't know how the matter was created, that merely explains one unknown in terms of another. Accident theories merely defer the explanation of biology to chemistry of elements, whose origins are also not known.

Religions also refer to a creator to explain life, but the creator is typically imagined as a life form, but if life forms existed before the beginning of life, then it cannot be the beginning. All such theories explain one unknown in terms of other unknowns, and create huge quantities of information, without answering any fundamental questions [91].

Our education system is inundated with such inconsequential debates that don't answer any significant questions. Consider sex education where debates range over safe sex versus abstention. No sex education class asks the simple question of why we have sex! It is almost a taboo to acknowledge that most sex in the western world is for the purpose of pure pleasure, with no reproductive intent. Sex for pleasure is fundamentally different from sex for reproduction, and it raises serious questions about who is entitled to that pleasure, when, and with what legal, financial, or emotional commitment. Existing rules and requirements all relate to reproductive sex, such as age compatibility, sufficient maturity and financial independence for parenthood, and attractiveness of the partner for a life-long exclusive bond to raise children. It is not clear what the rules need to be for hedonistic sex. It is probably none of the above, liberating sex from a plethora of unnecessary restrictions and taboos, and eliminating untold pain, suffering, and loneliness. Somehow, such fundamental questions are left to the individuals to figure out for themselves, but reams of information is generated on questions that are irrelevant or have no reliable answers [57].

Another similar and unusually complex issue in modern life is the concept of romantic love. Romantic love dominates our literature and our music. The energy spent on writing and singing about love, studying it, not to mention searching for it, is probably more than any other human endeavor, including food and shelter. One third of our adult life is spent on searching for a suitable romantic partner, and most of our adult leisure time is spent reading and singing about it [76]. Yet, such complexity brings little clarity to the subject. On the contrary, making things more complex then they need to be inhibits our understanding of them, and arriving at good solutions. Romantic love is treated as a supernatural force that is not amenable to analysis, but requires mere acceptance. We are told that you can't force it, define it, or control it, but you will know it when you find it. It will change you profoundly, and make you a new, better, and happier person. Yet the reality does not resemble this complex and supernatural story. Romantic love appears very much like an obsessive-compulsive disorder resulting from persistent sexual frustration and a profound fear of loneliness. That is not surprising since sexual frustration is the defining characteristic of modern life due to the changing definitions of marriage and socially approved sexual activity; and loneliness is a modern epidemic resulting from the collapse of the extended family and the weakening of religious and geographical communities. The super-natural euphoria experienced by lovers appears to be an anticipation of the end of sexual frustration and loneliness once and for all. It is also a self-fulfilling prophecy since the anticipation of supernatural feelings when the right partner is found triggers precisely those feelings when a partner is chosen as the right one. It at once justifies the choice of that partner and also fulfils the expectation of euphoria. Unfortunately, as one would expect from such unnatural and supernatural expectations, as soon as the sexual frustration and loneliness are relieved and immediate expectations are met, the supernatural feelings disappear, and they are replaced by the reality of disappointment, boredom, fear, and annoyance resulting from such extensive emotional dependence on another person. Supernatural expectations cannot survive long when contradicted by the experience of uncompromising reality. Yet, the social myth persists. Those who experience the loss of love blame themselves or their partners; and the rest struggle to find love. They all try to keep the myth alive, since once you commit yourself to the myth, your happiness depends on it. It is a self-justifying force fueled by the sexual frustrations of every new generation of young people; fed by the expectations created by music, movies, and literature; supported by the large number of people already committed to the idea as a source of their happiness; and most importantly, encouraged by the number of specialists and experts making a living at advising and counseling on how to live a good life filled with romantic love. The complexity created by such a pervasive myth chases away the simple truths about human sexuality and bonding.

Even romantic kissing, although non-reproductive and a rather routine and uncomplicated activity, is imbued with undue importance and supernatural qualities. The feelings it evokes are used to gauge the value of a relationship, or the long-term potential of a partner. The feelings of euphoria and being swept off one's feet by a first kiss are associated with the identification of the right partner. In fact, romantic kissing has a very practical purpose. It exposes one to the germs of the potential sex partner, and provides future immunity to each other's germs, just like a vaccination. This is especially important for women, as kissing progresses to sexual intercourse and then to pregnancy, an early exposure to the male partner's germs is critical to women's health. This is because pregnancy reduces the mother's immunity to protect the fetus from rejection, and an early exposure to the partner's germs is vital to maintaining a woman's health during the period of low-immunity pregnancy. It is no wonder then that women like romantic kissing much more than men. Their lives depend on it!

Human sexuality is not intrinsically complex, and it was not always as it is now. Before the myth of romantic love and the advent of personal choice, the dominant model was a marriage contract between families, and the individuals involved had little to do with the decision. The families made the decisions by using rather simple criteria for the compatibility of the families such as social, economic, and geographic status of the families. Once you were married, you had strict obligations to fulfil to your spouse, and to the families. The rules were strict and individual consent to each was not necessary. A 2008 Public Television program Frontline included an interview with a nomadic Mongolian family about their family life. The woman was complaining that she was overwhelmed with work because of breastfeeding the baby, heating the home, cooking, cleaning, and taking care of livestock. The interviewer pointed at her husband who was resting at the time, and asked why she wouldn't ask him for help. Her amazed reaction was typical of a traditional family, that it wasn't his job, he had his own job to do, and thousands of years of tradition had defined their roles in minute detail. Such strict roles are an anathema to modern families, but they have some serious advantages.

In societies where there are strict rules, roles, and a well-defined uniform lifestyle, it is much easier to find a compatible partner, and much easier to manage a lifelong relationship. More information, more variety, more freedom, and more choices make life much more difficult. Modern relationships provide few rules of behavior, but emphasize freedom of choice for everyone. But freedom and choice come at a high price of information and decision overload. Love, romance, consensual sex, reproductive choice, and shared housework are all rather recent developments, and they created an explosion of complex choices and decisions involving huge amounts of information. Numerous decisions have to be made, and each decision effects the partner, the children, the careers, and the extended families. Every decision has to be negotiated, and a consensus has to be reached among all involved, no matter how trivial the issue is. The issues range from critical to trivial, such as reproduction and health care, career moves and relocations, or cooking dinner and taking out the garbage. Is it any wonder then that most relationships collapse under the weight and stress of constant negotiation and debate? If there is beauty in simplicity, modern relationships are quite ugly!

Another heated debate in the US is about the mass shooters in schools; what motivates them, and why they target schools. There are many theories, and even more suggestions about possible solutions. Probably the least effective solution is to arm everyone so that they can defend themselves. In a crowded artificial environment of schools, churches, sports events, movie theaters, and shopping malls, that solution is likely to lead to a disaster, as the following cartoon sarcastically suggests [https://www.facebook.com/photo.php?fbid=10206565040822311&s et=a.2362470138743.2123435.1160032555&type=3&theater].
Another similar and humorous critique of this issue involves recommendations that everybody buy gorillas to defend themselves after a gorilla escapes from a zoo and viciously attacks some people [114].

The issue is actually remarkably simple. Almost all shooters have mental health problems. In a competitive society with a crumbling family structure, there is no unconditional love and acceptance. All emotional support comes conditionally, and only to those who deserve it, by being beautiful, articulate, pleasant, smart, and successful. Mentally ill often get shunned and rejected by all, although they need more support than everybody else. That combination of mental illness, and lack of social and emotional support is deadly, literally. In an environment full of guns, these angry, rejected, and mentally unstable people have some very deadly options; and in their desperation they sometimes make very bad and deadly decisions. This simple fact gets lost in unending political debates about gun rights, and violent content in video games and movies [109].

Decision making is a curse! Not only it is information intensive and complex, but humans are notoriously bad at it [7, 99]. We are experiencing increasing complexity and information overload not only in our personal lives but also in our professional careers. But it wasn't always so! Before industrial revolution, your family business was your business, and you were expected to follow the family tradition, whether it was farming, crafts, or business. Your family name often reflected the family business; for example, Smith being a blacksmith, and Clark being a cleric. Nobody was asked for their consent, and there were no decisions to be made. Now, career advice is big business, and a major part of any educational activity. The standard advice is to go into a line of work that you love. But the distinction between what you already love, and what you learn to love over time is always lost to career counselors, probably because it is impossible to predict what one will learn to love after being exposed to it for a considerable period of time. Conversely, it is not at all clear how you can possibly know what you love without being exposed to it in great detail, leading to a vicious cycle. This argument applies equally to romantic love.

To solve the problem of decision making, we increasingly rely on data collection, which leads to huge collections of data. But the more variables we observe, the more difficult the decisions become because of combinatorially increasing number of choices and interactions, and the more data we need to collect about those variables, in an unending vicious cycle. The so called "big data" problem is really a big decision problem with too many interacting variables. Increasingly, data is used to make mere predictions by using brute force computing, testing all possible correlations, with no theory, and no understanding of causal relationships underlying the predictions. Unexplained knowledge is no knowledge!

There are some success stories where unexplained knowledge can appear like real knowledge, but it can also fail unexpectedly and with no obvious explanation. IBM's supercomputer Watson plays the TV game Jeopardy with great success. It learns by reading encyclopedic documents on the web, and uses brute force computing to determine which phrases occur with which other phrases to discover relationships. But that is not real discovery, but merely aggregating quickly what other people already know. The writers of those documents put those terms together precisely because they know they are related. Using Watson to discover new relationships such as the causes of illnesses is likely to fail, although there are plans to use it for that purpose by reading medical records. Even if it could discover correlations among illnesses and possible causes, it will not be able to establish causality, and even if it could, it could not suggest any method of intervention without understanding the biological processes underlying that cause. Yet, it will generate a lot of unreliable spurious correlations that will confuse the public more than it educates.

Academic research is also increasingly complex. It now takes about six years to educate an academic researcher beyond college. Yet, the quality and the utility of research findings are increasingly marginal, because the problems are exponentially more complex. Elegant and insightful solutions of Newton, Freud, Darwin or Einstein are increasingly obsolete, as we delve into more detail, and find more exceptions and more mistakes in their analyses. The rough but general solutions are useful and insightful; the detailed and fine-tuned solutions are complex, yet provide no great insights. The forest gets buried under the trees, and research becomes a tedious and painstaking task with increasingly marginal contributions that are accurate to a fault. Scientists are constantly and accurately criticized for confusing accuracy and precision with significance. Typical research article now gets read by only a few people who are typically in the very narrow field as the author. The typical blog has exactly 1.5 readers: one is the author, and 0.5 is half of a significant other. When you can't even get the full significant other to read your blog, is it really worth writing it [73]?

Big data is likely to expand this problem into the world of business. Collecting huge amounts of data is the easy part. Making sense of it is hard! Large amounts of computing power will have to be dedicated to comb through these huge data sets which are typically unstructured with lots of text, video, and social media interactions. The result will often be little nuggets of information that are garnered at great cost. Will they be worth it if they improve your bottom line marginally? What if they come at a cost of losing insights about your business objectives, but instead shifting focus to customer tracking? There is a danger that your business focus might be transformed into collecting and analyzing data, instead of making shoes or pizza. This is not just a theoretical concern. A company like Nike is already more in the business of image creation and data analysis than it is in the business of making shoes. Nike does not make any shoes, but outsources all manufacturing to other companies in Asia. It focuses on marketing, design and collecting and analyzing customer data. With big data, this trend will intensify, and it will be in the business of customizing the image to each customer, and analyzing the data to target individual customers. The making of shoes by overseas companies will be increasingly disconnected from the main business of information analysis and image creation. With a flood of information about customers, the emphasis will shift increasingly from making better shoes to creating better images in the minds of consumers. More information about consumers invariably takes the attention away from the main business objective, and replaces it with information analysis and manipulation.

Constant monitoring of your customers leads to the "breaking news" phenomenon of the 24-hour news channels where the minute trivia dominate the attention, and replaces the slow deliberate contemplation of the larger issues and fundamental solutions. Businesses that are most responsive to customer comments are not necessarily the best businesses, because they react to each comment incrementally, rather than evaluating their overall goals and methods. Restaurants that are most responsive to customer complaints are not necessarily the best restaurants, because they react to each complaint individually, instead of searching for underlying problems. Teachers that are most responsive to student comments are not necessarily the best teachers, because improvements suggested by students are rarely the correct solutions to more fundamental problems, because students are good identifying problems, but not very good at suggesting solutions, since they are not in a good position to compare and contrast different ways of teaching. Monitoring your blood sugar levels constantly does not necessarily lead to a better management of your diabetes, since reacting to each fluctuation takes the attention away from long term solutions. Long term solutions require asking hypothetical questions. What happens if I change my business operations instead of just fixing a specific problem? That question cannot be answered by simply monitoring, because it relates to a hypothetical new situation, as opposed to what you have been monitoring. Short-term fixes to get immediate return are rarely the best long-term strategies. That is why businesses that are overly focused on quarterly returns rarely make the necessary long-term investments for long-term viability. That is why Amazon is an unusual company that almost never shows a quarterly profit, but constantly reinvests its earnings to revolutionize retail in the US. That rarely happens if the management is focused on constantly responding to investor sentiment and short term concerns. Should I fire the waiter who is receiving the most complaints from customers, or do I need to change the layout of the restaurant to make waiters more efficient? The latter question requires a lot more creative design than merely monitoring and collecting data. Should I add more jokes to my lectures because the students are complaining that my lectures are boring, or do I need to worry that the material I teach may not be challenging or relevant to their career goals? The former is the most likely response when constant evaluation of teaching becomes the norm, as opposed to designing fundamentally revolutionary courses when instructors that are given the freedom to experiment, instead of being shackled by the high-rating requirements every semester. Should I constantly watch what I eat by monitoring my glucose levels, or do I need to make more permanent changes in my lifestyle such as exercise, family life, or career choices? The latter requires asking hypothetical what if questions that cannot be answered by simply monitoring and responding to immediate concerns.

More importantly monitoring can change behavior, distorting the findings and responses. If you constantly evaluate teachers, they start teaching to the tests, and that may improve the evaluations, but may result in poor and narrow learning. Ironically, that may lead to even more stringent evaluation, leading to a vicious cycle where all creativity and experimentation is discouraged. If you constantly monitor teenagers, they might rebel against lack of privacy and take evasive behavior. Ironically, that leads to even more monitoring, until you get all out warfare between parents and their teenage children. Security cameras annoy citizens and lead to vandalism, which encourages even more security cameras to prevent vandalism, leading to a vicious cycle of increasing hostility between the government and its citizens. Monitoring and big data operations are dangerous because they change the focus and they change behavior in unexpected ways. They are classic examples of replacing minimal and intuitive information with unnecessarily complex large data sets.

There are similar concerns in the field of medicine. There is a great deal of excitement that big data about patients and their health outcomes might revolutionize medicine. Wearable sensors tracking patient health on a continuous basis, and patient records tracking the medical interventions and their outcomes universally, will be aggregated and analyzed with respect all relevant variables ranging from geography to demographics to health professionals involved. What is the rate of 5-year survival for all cardiac stent procedure patients of Dr. Clark, who are 60 year old males, diagnosed with high blood pressure, have two alcoholic drinks a day, and drive a BMW?! Big data technologies will make it possible to ask such questions easily, by the patients themselves, and directly from their phones and computers, and possibly with many more interesting but likely irrelevant factors. But will such complexity and sophistication help, or will it confuse the issues even more? Will they be worth it if they increase your life expectancy by a few minutes? What if they come at a cost of losing insights about the meaning of your life, and shifting your focus to s living longer? There is a danger that your focus may be transformed to collecting and analyzing data, instead of living a meaningful life. This is not just a theoretical concern. There is already too much focus on extending life as long as possible, irrespective of the quality of that life. There is some anecdotal evidence that doctors themselves are uncomfortable with the changing focus to extend life at any cost. They often refuse the end of life medical heroics for themselves as futile and dehumanizing, and die quickly and peacefully. Doctors may be dying differently from the rest of us, because they have first-hand knowledge of the misery and inhumanity caused by extending life at any cost. There is increasing discomfort in the medical community about bringing the cutting edge of technology to bear on a grievously ill person near the end of life. The patient will often get cut open, perforated with tubes, hooked up to machines, and assaulted with drugs. All of this occurs in the Intensive Care Unit at a cost of tens of thousands of dollars a day. What it buys is misery we would not inflict on a terrorist. There are many examples where attending physicians themselves say "if you ever find me in the situation of this patient, please kill me" [68].

With big data, this trend will intensify, and medicine will be increasingly about maximizing the life expectancy of each patient at any cost, by analyzing all the data about that patient. The simple quality of life questions will be increasingly disconnected from the complex business of extending life. With increasing complexity of medical procedures, the purpose of life suddenly becomes living a few months longer, rather than achieving a purpose. At some point, living longer becomes the only goal, irrespective of what you do with your life, and what quality of life you have. Quantity overwhelms quality, and the age-old simple wisdom about how to live a good life becomes obsolete, and it is replaced by the technologically complex question of how to live a longer life. With a flood of information about patients, the emphasis shifts increasingly from simple objective of improving the quality of life and comfort at the end, to complex and heroic measures to extend life. More information about patients invariably takes the attention away from the main objective of comforting them, and replaces it with information analysis and manipulation to improve measurable outcomes like life expectancy.

CHAPTER 3

FORMALITY

If you can't measure it, you can't control it; but if you measure it, you won't understand it.

Statistics is like a bikini. What it reveals is provocative; but what it hides is vital!

Formal tools are the backbone of modern science and education. Obsession with tools focuses attention on precision and accuracy, and often detracts from useful knowledge and fundamental truth. For example, the claim that earth is flat is wrong. The claim that earth is round is also wrong, but less so, because it is a more useful approximation for most applications. Obsession with precision and accuracy treats both of those claims as wrong, and loses useful knowledge in the process. Many religious myths are wrong. If you focus on accuracy and precision, you would be tempted to dismiss most religious myths as nonsense. If you focus on insight and usefulness, you can find that many myths are quite useful in guiding human behavior, explaining human condition using myths as metaphor, and even providing a glimpse into deeper truths about the purpose of life. Ignorance of formal facts and precise truths can even be a source of happiness. After all, facts are often ugly and depressing, and myths are beautiful, life enhancing, mood lifting, and mentally healing. Who would want to go through life with only ugly facts, but no utopian ideals and dreams as the following cartoon demonstrates [https://www.facebook.com/photo.php?fbid=10153328030726376&set=a.447536801375.246729.512686375&type=3&theater].

Formal and quantified information often leads to unjustified certainty and overconfidence since formality is often mistaken for quality. Such overconfidence can actually reduce the ability to search for truth and solve problems, by creating an illusion of certainty and expertise. Once formality is accepted as a substitute for correctness, at the expense of qualitative insight, measurement and quantification can become a panacea, dominate all analysis, and can lead to an explosion of quantitative information. Quantification and formality increases confidence a lot more than competence, leading to a vicious cycle of increasing reliance on measurement and quantification, as lack of competence causes frequent failures. The more you fail, the more you try to measure and quantify; the more you measure and quantify, the more you fail!

After every financial crisis, there is wide spread criticism of the financial models and their shortcomings. 2008 financial meltdown was no exception. Many economists and bankers, including the two chairmen of the Federal Reserve Bank at that time period, Alan Greenspan and Ben Bernanke, apologized profusely for not forecasting the crisis, and not dealing with it promptly, because of the failure of various formal financial models. But the solutions they put forward always involve more models and more formal analysis, perpetuating the problem in a vicious cycle. Failures are very profitable for economists and bankers, after a period of head scratching and self-examination. They generate an unending need for solutions to the very failures they caused. In general, scientists and professionals often profit handsomely from the very crises they precipitate with the failures of their models, by mitigating and repairing the damages they themselves caused. Mathematical models are even more useful to scientists when they fail, than when they succeed, simply because the failure generates a need for more foolproof models which are more difficult to discover and more difficult to analyze, creating more jobs and more job security for scientists [62].

Education is the biggest culprit in excessive formalization. And it starts with preschool. Formal education is increasingly replacing free play as a learning tool, with dire consequences in psychological health of children. There is growing suspicion among educators that maybe formal education at that age is all wrong! Maybe we just need to allow them to play, and learn naturally as our ancestors did, instead of constantly expanding formal education. As parents and teachers strive to provide increasingly organized learning experiences for children, the opportunities for free play, especially outdoors is becoming less of a priority. Ironically, it is through active free play outdoors, children start to build many of the foundational life skills they need in order to be successful in adulthood. When children reach elementary school, we practice special breathing techniques, coping skills, run social skill groups, and utilize special exercises in an attempt to teach children how to be still and to improve focus. However, these skills shouldn't have to be taught formally, but they should be developed at a young age through natural and meaningful play experiences. This might also apply to the education of college students and beyond. We may have lost our ability to learn through unstructured and pleasurable play and experimentation, and may be relying too much on formal, unpleasant and ineffective education, simply because it is easier to measure and quantify, with negative consequences for all involved at all educational levels [91]. The following cartoon aptly demonstrates the negative consequences of excessive formal education, and the following burnout, not only for students, but even for the teachers [https://www.facebook.com/JordanJansenMusic/photos/a.10150383755 079588.374852.233745389587/10152826681324588/?type=1&theater]. Similarly, the following cartoon demonstrates the apathy on the part of the students to excessive formal education and their skepticism about its usefulness [https://www.facebook.com/photo.php?fbid=10153734160362012&set =a.387707607011.166652.587027011&type=3&theater].

Contrast that to the joy of learning displayed by these youngsters learning to dance Samba in Brazil in the following video. No formal dance lessons are required [https://38.media.tumblr.com/1820ae3d268a2a5cab7fcbd71c9a0070/t umblr_nvjzza3JjT1rakka3o1_250.gif].

Education increases confidence a lot more than it increases competence, especially when it is adorned with degrees, awards, and prizes. It is hard not to feel confident and competent when everybody around you praises your accomplishments. Consequently, highly educated people, surrounded by other like-minded people, often suffer from overconfidence, especially in fields other than their narrow expertise. They may be even less reliable than less educated people who recognize their shortcomings. The inability to recognize one's own limitations is called Dunning-Kruger effect named after two Cornell psychologists, and it is widely known; but education which is largely accepted as a solution might actually make it worse [7]!

The issue is so pressing that there is even a new field of study that formally studies human ignorance, along with our ignorance of that ignorance! Agnotology, the study of ignorance, is a new field of study that highlights the fact that we often exaggerate how much we know, and deemphasize our ignorance. This is especially true in education and research, but also in politics, economics, medicine, and social issues. To complete the irony, it is unlikely that we know enough about ignorance itself to justify a formal field either! The study of ignorance or agnotology, a term popularized by Robert N. Proctor, a historian of science at Stanford is in its infancy. This emerging formal field of inquiry is fragmented because of its relative novelty and cross-disciplinary nature. But giving due emphasis to unknowns, highlighting case studies that illustrate the fertile interplay between questions and answers, and exploring the psychology of ambiguity are critical to understanding the extent of our ignorance hidden behind a cloak of formality [44, 62].

Consider driver training for hazardous road conditions. There is evidence that those who receive formal training for driving on snow and ice actually have higher accident rates than those who do not. That is probably because training increases confidence and leads to more risky driving, but it doesn't have a lasting impact on competence. Any skills acquired during training are lost very quickly, unless one practices them regularly. Since regular practice of driving on ice and snow is not feasible for most drivers, the increase in confidence far outstrips the increase in competence, leading to a worse accident record [96].

Formal education in general is mostly about confidence building, rather than teaching skills for specific jobs. That is why liberal arts education is often characterized as building citizenship and character. This is true even at the highest level of education aimed at building expertise in a narrow area. Political scientist Phillip Tetlock conducted experiments with political science experts and ordinary people to test their ability to make political predictions. Experts were much worse in predicting outcomes, yet they were much more confident in their ability to predict. That is because expertise gave them confidence, but also locked them into their favorite pet theories, and introduced more bias into their analyses. Educated people are also more prone to political propaganda because they simply read more of it as part of their education and literacy. The claim that President Obama is a Moslem is believed more by college educated people than high school graduates [97]. Supreme Court Justice Stephen Bryer famously recounts how ill-prepared he felt for the job when he was first appointed to the US Supreme Court. Yet after a few months on the job training, he felt confident enough to question the competence of other justices. His short experience probably did not increase his competence, but gave a big boost to his confidence, and made him more aggressive. This is the danger of education. It fosters a false sense of competence and makes us intellectually more aggressive [66, 98].

Increasing education does not solve the problem; it exacerbates it. In a famous experiment, subjects were given a balanced analysis of the climate change problem with all the evidence, and pros and cons of various actions carefully presented. Everybody had stronger opinions about climate change after the presentation, but only reinforcing their preexisting beliefs. Nobody changed their minds, but everybody became more confident. The more they studied, the stronger their biases got, because of ever increasing confidence, rising much faster than increasing knowledge [98].

Numbers and statistical reasoning make matters worse by creating certainty and precision when they are not justified. Numbers oversimplify facts, obscure complexity, and make hidden choices; and as such they rarely illuminate. Statistics is like a bikini. What it reveals is exciting and provocative; but what it hides is critical and vital! Consider IQ tests. They take a complex multidimensional trait like intelligence, and reduce it to a single number. They could be useful as a measurement of a very specific and narrow trait, like the ability to manipulate abstract symbols very

quickly, but their narrow assumptions are often ignored, and they are used as a general measure of competence and merit. They determine who gains access to educational resources and jobs, and consequently to economic and social advancement. They are used to economically and socially stratify society, and decide who will be allowed to climb up the social hierarchy and who will be left behind to do the low paying and menial jobs. In many countries with a military draft, IQ tests and related educational performance were used to decide who will get a comfortable desk job in the military, and who would go to the front lines to fight and die! In the US, only the top performing 2% of college students can qualify for admittance to a medical school. It is reasonable to ask if it is necessary to be in the top 2% to perform well in a medical school and become a good doctor, or is it an arbitrary criterion used to block access to the masses and limit the supply of doctors to maintain high salaries [47].

There are similar problems in journalism in comparing formal data-based stories versus narrative based stories. "The danger with stories based on numbers is that they can come out feeling too neat, as if the complexity and messiness of the real world can be reduced to mere data. This is why journalists publish a mix of stories that aim to capture the world in a variety of modes. Data-journalism is one of those modes, and it's a useful one, so long as you're aware that it can't tell a complete story all on its own. There will always be a huge amount of complexity and heterogeneity within a data set" [93].

Statistics is readily amenable to manipulation, and all social and political movements manipulate statistics to skew them in their direction. Some women's groups claim that there is a rape culture that approves and even encourages violence against women. The statistic that is often cited claims that one out of three women will be raped in her lifetime. It is hard to believe that statistic since most people do not think one of their three female friends will be raped in her lifetime. It turns out that statistic produced by independent researchers and reported widely by the FBI is clearly misleading in the pursuit of a political agenda. The researchers asked female subjects if they "ever engaged in sex although they did not want to", and one out of three answered yes. But that is hardly the common definition of rape, as people get pressured into sex by their loved ones or even casual acquaintances all the time, and do not ordinarily think of that as rape.

It is actually surprising that only one out of three answered yes to that question, as most people get pressured into sex sometime in their life, or do it for the benefit of their partner even when they don't feel like it. More interestingly, about the same percentage of male subjects answered yes to the same question, but that fact is never publicized. Clearly, if that is the definition of rape, males are raped by females as often as females being raped by males, and that also is not consistent with the common expectation and experience. Similarly, there is a wide spread claim that one out of five teenagers will be bullied online. Once again, the researchers asked the teen subjects if they "ever received an unwanted criticism or insult online". But that is hardly the common definition of bullying. It is surprising that only one in five ever received a criticism or insult online, since teens spend a huge chunk of their lives online. Similarly, women's groups have claimed that a woman earns 76 cents for every dollar earned by a man. But that statistic might be misleading because it doesn't consider that women might be more likely to spend more time on housework and be compensated indirectly for that work through their husbands. After all, those women who do full time housework earn zero dollars for every dollar a man earns, but one would not consider homemakers destitute, as they get paid indirectly through their husbands in the informal economy. Even more strikingly, there is wide spread acceptance that domestic violence is primarily committed by men against women. That is because overwhelming majority of domestic violence calls to the police comes from women against the men in their lives. But that statistic might be misleading, because when men are subject to domestic violence by the women in their lives, they are much less likely to call the police, because it is not socially acceptable for a man not to be able to take care of himself when subjected to violence by a woman. In fact, the statistics by social workers show that domestic violence is committed equally both by men and women. Once again, the researchers appear to be biased with specific political agendas or preconceived notions, and they pick and choose the numbers that support their agendas. Formality and statistics makes it easy to push such biases from mere opinion to respectable and neutral sounding research findings [28, 53, 111].

Consider the statistics that show that the life expectancy of humans have been rising steadily since the invention of agriculture. Here is a typical story about life expectancy that hides the reality behind numbers: Two cavemen are chatting. One tells the other: "Something isn't right. Our air is clean; our water is pure; we get plenty of exercise; everything we eat is organic and free range; yet nobody lives past 30." Something is wrong alright, and that is the statistics. Life expectancy at birth may have been accurately and precisely 30, but that is still very misleading, because it doesn't mean people die at around the age of 30. The life expectancy among hunter-gatherers at 45 was 23 more years of life, bringing it 68, closer to current levels. The reason for low life expectancy at birth was high rates of infant mortality, and also infanticide. Babies were not considered fully human, and disabled ones were probably killed. Average life expectancy across diverse cultures is not very meaningful, because the definition of human life varies. If you include the sperm in the computation, the life expectancy will go down to seconds; and if you include the people who can be kept in a vegetative state for decades, the life expectancy will rise dramatically, as it has more recently [85].

Similarly, it has been argued that our modern lives are much less violent than any other time in history. Those statistics are misleading.

First of all it is not clear what violence means. They certainly don't include the psychological violence we prefer to inflict on people such as prisoners, overweight, and the ugly. Second, it is not clear where and when the decline occurred. The level of physical violence vary greatly among geographical locations and time periods. Dresden and Hiroshima during the Second World War was probably more violent than anything our ancestors ever experienced or even imagined. Averaging those out with the wealthy and peaceful suburbs of America gives a distorted view of what people experience. Violence is localized in the modern world to war zones and poor urban slums. Third, a large world population distorts the violence statistics. One cannot simply look at percentages and gain insights. Otherwise, the Biblical record of Abel killing Caine, when the world population was 4, amounts to a violent death rate of 25%, and it would be equivalent to over 2 billion deaths today. Amount of violence is better measured by absolute numbers in specific locations and time, to reflect what is experienced by those people. Statistics in the form of averages is a main source of highly precise information that prevents insight and understanding [78, 95].

More importantly, it is not at all clear if civilization is the cause of the decline in violence, or if they simply happen to correlate for some other reason. Even if we accept that violence has declined with civilization, it is not clear why, and the reasons are critical for drawing the right conclusions. Without an explanation, statistics are often misleading, and lead to the unjustified conclusions and wrong policy recommendations. The simplest conclusion may not be the right one: that civilization reduces violence, so let's have more civilization! Violence studies provide a wonderful example of what is wrong with scientific findings. A great deal of effort is spent on the accuracy and the precision of the facts asserted; yet the significance and the policy implications of the findings are always implied with a nudge and a wink. Those are always non-scientific and often wrong. The facts are relatively clear: violence has decreased with civilization. The policy conclusions drawn are likely to be wrong: let's have more civilization to decrease violence even more. That conclusion requires the establishment of causality, not mere accidental correlation.

Even if we assume that the obvious implied explanation is correct, and that civilization makes us more moral, more conscious of the collective well-being, so more civilization is good for reducing violence; that immediately begs the next question. Does it make us more moral towards everybody, or only towards other civilized people? Native Americans, African Zulus, Middle Eastern Bedouins, and Australian Aborigines may not agree that civilization made us less violent. Maybe we have less violence on average, but more violence concentrated on specific groups. Then civilization may not be good for everyone, or only for those who benefit from it. Averages don't tell the whole story!

Another explanation could be that violence has declined because modern weapons are more deadly which discourages routine violence, but increases the risk of catastrophic violence when it finally occurs. The average violence declines but only by taking increasing risk. That explanation suggests that the reduction is only temporary, and the risk eventually catches up with you, and raises the averages. More importantly, there are incentives to constantly take more risk to reduce violence, by developing even more deadly weapons to discourage violence. But that is a pyramid scheme, and a vicious cycle, because the need for increasing risk at each step to reduce violence eventually leads to catastrophic violence, all the while social scientists praising the virtues of civilization in reducing violence. This is precisely what happened before the two world wars! The world's intellectuals were overwhelmingly convinced that with such deadly weaponry, a war in Europe was unthinkable, and with civilization and modern technologies, the age of unending wars between empires had finally come to an end. Yet, the two world wars devastated the civilized Europe. Identifying the real explanations for statistical observations is critical to drawing the right conclusions.

Yet another explanation for the observed reduction in violence is that physical violence may have been converted to psychological violence, because people are valuable and controllable resources in an industrial society, so you enslave them instead of killing them. Prisons are quintessential examples of psychological punishment and violence, replacing an earlier model of executing or maiming criminals. Prison is a show designed to objectify and dehumanize the criminal. Once upon a time, killing and torture were the common punishments. They modified the physical body of the criminal. Prisons modify the mind. At a time when people communicated with their physical presence and their body, killing and torture may have been effective, and many creative ways were invented to send the message forcefully. Serbian rulers, in the Middle Ages, perfected a technology where a long stick was inserted into the whole length of a criminal's body, from anus to mouth, but without killing him, and then he was exhibited to the general public in the town square with the stick in him for several days, as he slowly died. Roman crucifixion, Chinese water torture, European guillotines, and Middle Eastern amputations all had the same effect. The body was altered, objectified, torn to pieces, and eliminated [12].

As technologies changed, and people started communicating remotely, through writing and printing, and later by electronic communication, killing was not as effective, since the ideas continued to propagate. One has to control the mind to take away the power of ideas. Prisons are invented for this purpose, where the prisoners continue to communicate with the outside world, and try to prove that they changed their behavior, and they are remorseful. This is called rehabilitation. However, with ever increasing power of formal communication technologies, prisons may have lost their effectiveness to modify minds. Prison is a show for the outsiders, and as such the biggest danger is inmate defiance. But it is difficult to make prison a show, where outsiders can look in, without insiders looking out. Consequently, not having complete control of prisoners' information intake, allows them to create a prison culture by importing some of their outside ideas into the prison. If prisoners can set the norms and enforce the rules of behavior, as opposed to the prison system and the guards, then a criminal culture is created inside the prison and forces everyone to conform. The prison becomes an institution of counterculture, a criminal education enterprise, with results quite contrary to its stated objectives [30].

Prison as a reeducation system is most prominently displayed in a rare experiment in Iran, where convicts were sentenced to buy and read certain books and demonstrate their understanding of the concepts.
This might be the only official acknowledgement of reading as punishment, but it also demonstrates the purpose of prison as a communication system that forces the prisoners to acknowledge their mistakes and influence others through their repentance [11].

The modern prison as a formal structure of punishment was invented by Jeremy Bentham in 1791. He called it Panapticon. Prison as punishment was a radical concept, since previously prisons were mere temporary holding places before a trial or execution. In his design, prisoners are prevented from interacting with each other, by placing them in permanent solitary confinement, in cells placed around a circular courtyard. But they are always observed by the guards in a tower in the center of the courtyard. The observation tower had one-way glass so the prisoners could not even see the guards, but they were always under observation because their cell had a glass wall facing the courtyard. This design accomplished the objective of allowing no privacy and exercising complete control with the existing technologies of the time. Bentham's architecture was never implemented. But modern technologies of cameras and sensors make his dream of no privacy and complete control much more practical. Cameras are already being deployed in a large scale in urban areas and also in the phones of fellow citizens, to take away privacy [73]. Privacy was always a problem as the following funny cartoon demonstrates, with norms enforced by human eyes, but cameras and the resulting surveillance society take it to an unprecedented level [https://www.facebook.com/531471026925998/photos/a.6385858462 14515.1073742317.531471026925998/944738328932597/?type=1&t heater],

Sensors and sensor networks will take away the remaining privacy, by monitoring citizens even when they are away from cameras and other people. Modern urban life is also increasingly isolating physically, because of the mobility created by transportation technologies and global economies. As a result of mobility, and a lack of permanent group identification, our information intake is increasingly controlled by electronic media as opposed to face to face contact. Controlling those media would accomplish Bentham's dream of information control in a large scale. Bentham already suggested that this architecture was applicable, not just to prisons, but to all institutions such as the military, schools, hospitals, even families, where controlling people's minds in addition to their bodies was critical.

But one has to be very careful, since with great power comes great responsibility. Humans are social animals, and need privacy and control over their information to have personal identities. There is evidence from monkey experiments that monkeys that are isolated, and strictly controlled, become anti -social and even schizophrenic in short order. In an effort to control the society with formal structures, we always risk the danger of creating wide-spread mental illness. Already there are epidemics of depression, attention deficit disorder, and autism in the Western World; and our high-tech lifestyle with its physical isolation of the individual, electronic communication, and fragmented social life are suggested as possible culprits. If we are simply replacing physical violence with psychological violence, simply because it is more effective to control behavior, more civilization is not necessarily optimum. Simply decreasing physical violence without understanding the impact of its replacement, psychological violence, may prove to be more dangerous and more detrimental to human health and well-being than ever [71].

A final possible explanation for the reduction of violence is that violence against humans is being replaced by violence against other species and nature. By exploiting other species and the wild nature more effectively, we can reduce competition with and violence against other humans, because the competition for resources shifts from taking away resources from other humans to taking then away from other species. Exterminating other species that don't serve human interests, and converting their habitat to human objectives reduces violence among humans, both because of additional resources making violence less necessary, but also because the energy required for violence being redirected, and the violence against other species and nature requiring more cooperation among humans to be effective. Nature as the common enemy merely unites humans more effectively. But violence against other species and nature also creates risk, as discussed above, because nature has complex interconnecting webs of interdependence, and eliminating some species can have unexpected consequences on human species through indirect connections; and these unexpected consequences may take long years to develop. It is very dangerous then to draw the formal statistical conclusion that more civilization means less human suffering without understanding those intricate web of connections and long term risks of reduced human violence.

Formal analysis largely relies on averages and expected outcomes. But averages are misleading because very few people are actually average. The average income in the United States is 28,000 dollars. But very few people actually make exactly 28,000 dollars, so any analysis about the purchasing power of 28,000 dollars is really relevant to just a few people. This is also a fundamental problem with online rating systems that are commonly used to measure quality. Trip Advisor publishes the average ratings of all restaurants and hotels. But average ratings are correct only if all raters are equally competent to judge, and even then they are only relevant to the average consumer. It treats all ratings equally and averages them out, ignoring the differences between raters, their biases, preferences, and qualifications; and then presents the same rankings to all consumers, ignoring the differences in their biases and preferences. A highly rated Italian restaurant rarely has the best lasagna, and to someone only interested in lasagna, the average ratings are irrelevant! Similarly, college ratings are published every year by US News and World Report magazine. It is not clear why all raters should be counted equally; and more importantly, it is not clear who these ratings are for. An average college student, with an average major, average interests, average intelligence, and average capability in every endeavor, probably does not exist. Maybe the ratings are close enough for most people, but for those with more specific interests and qualities, average ratings can be terribly misleading.

There is increasing reliance on ratings and recommendations to find high quality products and service providers. Ratings and recommendations may be highly unreliable, even for the average consumer, so much so that the worst-rated service providers may in fact be the best. Consider two surgeons: one working in upper-east-side of Manhattan and doing elective surgery, and the other in a safety net hospital in North Philadelphia and operating mainly on high-risk patients. Their ratings will be dramatically different whether they are based on informal patient comments or official morbidity rates. Operating on high-risk patients in an overcrowded North Philadelphia hospital is not comparable to operating in upper-east-side of Manhattan on wealthy elective surgery patients. Even if the former is the more skilled surgeon, his ratings and performance measures will be considerably lower. The most ambitious and best skilled surgeons who take on such big challenges may very well be the worst-rated surgeons. How can you make good decisions based on performance measures and consumer ratings then? It is almost impossible to have reliable ratings and recommendations for professional service providers. Professionals need to be rated and evaluated by other professionals who can judge the quality of work, not by the general public, and not by the statistical performance measures that simply look at outcome. This problem is common with all professionals from teachers to lawyers. Teachers that teach in inner city schools are likely to have much worse performance measures or student evaluations that those who teach in wealthy suburbs, because the audience is different and resource availability is different. Lawyers who take on very difficult cases as public defenders are much more likely to fail, than personal injury lawyers who pick and choose the cases they take, on the basis of winnability. Academics who take on big and high impact projects are much more likely to fail and be rated low than the academics who take on small inconsequential but easily publishable projects. That is why new faculty members are often advised not to "bite more than they can chew" and not to take on big and serious research projects, but instead build a track record with smaller projects [49].

Professionals need to be evaluated informally by other professionals with the same expertise, instead of relying on formal measures of ratings and outcomes. But then there is the problem of a few experts in a narrow field rating each other very highly, even if the field itself is not terribly useful, or fail to produce high quality work. This happens in some of the new academic fields. Those who don't quite measure up to the high standards of an old established academic field like sociology, splinter and start a new subfield like family studies where the standards may not be as stringent. It is very difficult to evaluate the field itself as it is rather specialized, and the evaluation of individuals is done by others in that field who may not have high standards. Professionals are very difficult to evaluate. If you rely on their peers, they may not be of high quality. If you rely on others, they may not be relevant. This is a paradox of evaluation.

Statistical analysis in social sciences also focuses on a typical or average subject, but very few people are actually typical or average, so the results may not apply perfectly to most people. Average marriage lasts seven years, but that may not be relevant to most people who do not have average marriages. The expected value does not tell us why and under what conditions the expected duration might change, and there may be infinitely many such conditions and factors in evaluating the risk in any particular marriage. More importantly, the expected value doesn't tell us the worst case scenarios, and under what conditions they might take place. Vague but intuitive insights into marriages and what makes them fail in general may be more useful than the expected duration, or even the variance, since they can provide vague but relevant policy guidelines by inferring causality [1, 95]

Consider the statistical finding that children who grow up with two parents are healthier and more successful in life. The immediate and obvious policy conclusion is to support the marriage institution and to discourage divorce. In fact, that might be the wrong policy conclusion without further insight. One needs to understand why people divorce and how that affects children, which is called the process or domain knowledge. For example, it is possible that if you separate good marriages and bad marriages, the children of bad marriages may be better off after a divorce. If you distinguish between amicable divorces and hostile divorces, the children of amicable divorces may be healthier and more successful than the children of married couples. And those are just two simple examples. There are infinitely many such variables that may allow fine tuning of any statistical analysis, such that without a detailed qualitative understanding of the divorce process and how it affects children, it would be difficult to draw a policy conclusion from a purely statistical analysis. Without such insight, calculating the risk to children from divorce would be too general to be useful, or even fundamentally incorrect [37, 77].

Statistics and expected values are even more misleading with rare but catastrophic events. Rare event are difficult to predict accurately; impossible to predict if they have never happened before. Yet that doesn't stop economists, meteorologists, engineers, and urban planners from producing large amounts of predictive analysis for disasters, even if it is not terribly useful. The philosopher Bertrand Russell tells the story of a statistician turkey to demonstrate the folly of disaster prediction. There once was a very smart turkey, highly educated in statistics. He lived on a beautiful farm run by a loving farmer. He was surrounded by many turkey friends, and his days were filled with joy, eating, sleeping, having sex, and frolicking in the fields with friends. Of course, there were some disturbing rumors of the farmer killing turkeys for no reason, so just to make sure, he meticulously collected data about the health and welfare of all the turkeys on the farm. To his pleasant surprise, he found that there were very few deaths and disappearances, and they were all probably due to illness and injury, according to his records and analysis. Every day he collected data and performed statistical analysis; and every day his confidence increased that the farmer was a loving man who cared for his turkeys very much, and watched for their best interest. Then, just when his confidence reached almost certainty, Thanksgiving came!!! The story demonstrates the difficulty of predicting rare events, yet the critical importance of rare but catastrophic events on future performance. After all, if you can't survive a single rare but catastrophic event, the expected values are not terribly useful. Expected values are useful in repeated experiments, but to the airline passenger who dies in that rare airplane crash, the fact that planes are safer than taxicabs is no consolation and terribly irrelevant.

There is wide-spread agreement that air travel is safer than automobile travel. The statistics show that more people die in automobile accidents than in airplane accidents. But that fact alone may not be very meaningful. First of all there are more miles travelled by car than by plane, so the accident rates have to be normalized to per mile travelled. But that may not be meaningful either, since a typical car trip is much shorter than a plane trip, so normalizing the accident rates per trip may be more appropriate. But that will only help if planes and automobiles are actually available as alternatives for a given trip. They are not always. A trip to the grocery store cannot be taken by plane; or the trip to Europe cannot be taken by car; so the relative safety is not a meaningful concept for those trips. But how do we compare different modes of transportation in terms of safety then? Relative safety can only be relevant when we are comparing two modes of transportation for a particular trip to decide which mode to take. The fact that there are lots of accidents in the grocery store parking lot is not relevant to the decision involving a European trip. One would need to make the comparison for comparable trips where the alternatives are available. Even if a careful analysis could resolve all of these issues, the average accident rates may not be relevant to a particular traveler. The average accident rates apply to an average driver and an average pilot, but very few drivers are actually average. Some are better drivers; some are worse. Their results would be very different from the average driver. Although fliers do not have a choice of their pilot, so relying on the average accident rates may be reasonable for them; drivers control their own destiny, and the quality of drivers may be much more variable than the quality of commercial pilots, so the average rates may not be very reliable for them. Finally, to make the comparison almost impossible, safety technologies are not static. Every new model of a car, and every new generation of planes have new safety technologies;

not to mention the changes to highway safety, road design, police presence, airport design, air traffic control technologies, radar equipment on the planes, automatic collision avoidance technologies, and a plethora of other technologies change the relevant factors. In a highly technological and fast changing society, past statistics are almost never relevant to future events. Yet, we are bombarded with such statistics daily [37, 95].

Adding to the difficulty, statistical analysis focuses on expected risk, not the risk of extremes and catastrophes. Gamblers for example often calculate their odds of winning, but the expected value may not be very useful. Even if the expected value was positive, most gamblers end up losing against the house, because when the oscillations between wins and losses are large, most people quit when they run out of money. Of course, that is exactly the wrong time to quit, but a gambler with limited funds has no choice. A good example of this is the "sure win" strategy that is often espoused by roulette players. The idea is to simply double your bet after every loss, and start over after every win. If winning pays double, then your expected winnings are always positive, as long as you don't quit immediately after a loss, but double down as your strategy requires. Yet, most people lose anyway, because you need a large sum of money to be able to continue doubling your bet, and when you run out of money, you can't continue. So, the critical risk is the risk of a catastrophe, which is running out of funds, not the expected risk by playing indefinitely [95].

The gambling example has many real world analogs. Nassim Taleb argues in his book *The Black Swan* that this is a fundamental problem in financial markets where expected risk and return is commonly used to evaluate investments. But the rare financial crises may be the determining factor for most investors and businesses. Such rare events are rarely factored into risk/return calculations, because they are difficult to predict, and even impossible if they have never happened before. Yet, they could be devastating to investors and businesses, since a single crisis can force them out of the market after a big loss, and at precisely the wrong time to quit. He gives as an example the impossibility of predicting the existence of a black swan, since in Europe all swans were white, until black swans were discovered in Australia. A black swan type of crisis, which has never been seen before, is impossible to predict. Similarly, financial engineering technologies are constantly introducing new financial instruments that create new risks of catastrophe. They are impossible to predict, because they have never happened before, since those technologies did not exist before. Consequently, past average returns may not be relevant to investors; but they might be much better advised to invest with the goal of avoiding financial catastrophes that may be the deciding factor for long term returns. NYU professor Nassim Taleb runs an investment fund precisely with that contrarian objective where he routinely loses money, but makes huge profits in the event of a financial crisis. Yet, forecasting financial crises is almost impossible; and past performance continues to dominate all the financial statistics and guide all investment decisions [95].

More importantly, statistical analysis focuses on precision and correctness in a narrow domain, and under strict assumptions, at the expense of intuitive concepts and general principles that are roughly correct but apply broadly. The precision and reliability of analytical models become liabilities if they lead to overconfidence and overgeneralization. Specificity and precision do not imply broad applicability. On the contrary, analytical models are often very brittle, and when their (not necessarily realistic) assumptions are not satisfied, they can fail dramatically. Moreover, the abstractions of the analytical models increase the opaqueness of their assumptions, and raise the danger of overgeneralizing. Broad qualitative insights on the other hand are often roughly correct and lack precision, but apply more generally and with fewer and more transparent assumptions. For example, during the 2008 financial crisis, former Federal Reserve chairman Alan Greenspan famously acknowledged that the financial markets had failed to obey some basic assumptions made in their analytical models, such as markets self-correcting, and banks accurately judging their own long term self-interest. Without those basic assumptions, most analytical models could not reliably predict market behavior, even in the aggregate. With constantly changing financial engineering technologies, the ability to predict the behavior of financial markets, and to judge the impact of specific Federal Reserve actions is even more suspect [56, 95].

Similarly, extreme and rare rewards are often ignored in statistical models, but in fact they might be the primary driver of human behavior. This might be the reason why people buy lottery tickets, although their chances of winning are very low, and the expected value of the ticket is always less than the cost. But money does not have linear utility. The value of a large win is so high that it dominates the decision process. This is the same reason why people commit property crimes, although they are likely to be caught and punished, and the expected value of the crime is less than the cost of punishment. But the value generated from crime can be so high in the rare case of not being caught, or in the brief period before being caught, that it dominates the decision process, especially because the cost of punishment comes later and gradually over a long period of jail time. Especially for those whose lives are not very rewarding and meaningful, the cost of punishment may be minimal, since a prison life may not be terribly different from a difficult life in a crowded and dangerous inner city slum. Even the death penalty may not be a deterrent for someone with a dismal life, if the reward can be a life changing experience, at least briefly. Crimes of passion, sex crimes, drug crimes, property crimes all have this quality; and punishment may not be an effective deterrent, as high rates of recidivism also confirm. Punishment for crime may be merely an opportunity to take revenge and to get psychological satisfaction. If the purpose of punishment is deterrence, the system of punishment has to be reassessed, as technologies of crime change the rewards and risks, but also the technologies of crime prevention such as monitoring and tracking become more effective. Deterrence requires an emphasis on prevention, not punishment after the fact. Yet our justice system is largely preoccupied with punishment, and measures effectiveness as the ability to punish offenders and to reduce recidivism, because it is easier to measure formally. It is not focused on preventing crime in the first place, because that would be difficult to measure and formalize. [7, 51].

Economic statistics similarly hide important insights. GDP is a measure of the total value of the goods produced by a nation, and it is often used as a measure of wealth. But by that measure, primitive and more traditional societies are often deemed poor, because they rely partly on non-cash economies with bartered or shared resources. By the same reason, development always seems to increase wealth, despite the immense poverty and suffering it creates in some parts of the world.

According to this measure of wealth, if the river is clean, and everybody freely drinks the river water, that doesn't contribute to the wealth of a nation; but if the river is polluted, and everybody has to buy bottled water for cash, that is included in the wealth of a nation, and considered growth. If everybody is mentally healthy with vibrant communities and extended families, that does not contribute to the wealth of a nation, and it is considered poverty; but when the mental health of a community declines, and people pay cash to get help from professionals, that contributes to the cash economy, and considered growth and wealth. These are perverse measures of wealth and growth, yet their precision and technical accuracy hide the perverse assumptions that lead to misleading conclusions [33].

CHAPTER 4

SOLUTIONS

Substitution is an institutional problem, because it is the social institutions such as governments, businesses, markets, schools, and churches that generate the bulk of the information consumed by the public. Institutions have an incentive to create cheap information for short-term efficiency, complex information to protect their bureaucracies, and formal information to manage and control their bureaucracies, and in the process they replace high quality information with cheaper, more complex, and more formal but lower quality information. There are two fundamental solutions to such dysfunctional institutions. One is to increase their flexibility so that they can adjust to the changing environment faster, more efficiently, and with less conflict, reducing the need for them to impose on the general public their own self-serving information content. Second is to create a diversity of social institutions that compete with each other, and to prevent the monopolization of social life by specific institutions. The two solutions are not independent, and may in fact be complementary, since competition may force institutions to become more flexible, and flexibility may make them more competitive.

Social institutions are critical to social organization and stability. Governments, businesses, markets, military, schools, hospitals, families, and churches are all complex institutions, designed to provide a multitude of services to their constituencies, through an elaborate system of social organization. They employ permanent bureaucracies to provide stability and reliability in the creation and delivery of those services. Yet, the stability they aim to provide makes them inflexible, and in a rapidly changing technology-laden environment, leads to large scale substitution of their institutional interests for the public good. The dichotomy between stability and flexibility has been an enduring debate among social scientists. The classic problem of choosing between buying and leasing of resources in economics, the long standing controversy between government and business in political science, and the unending debate between markets and hierarchies in organizational sociology are all examples of this dichotomy. In all of these dichotomies, both solutions have advantages and disadvantages, leading to protracted philosophical debates on how to evaluate those advantages and disadvantages. But recently, new information technologies created new possibilities to resolve these long standing conflicts in creative ways, by eliminating the rigid rules that govern these institutions with respect to the ownership of resources, membership in institutions, and permanence of bureaucracies [9, 106].

It is now possible to have an ownership mechanism for resources that is not absolute, where institutions and even individuals can share resources with others, and have limited rights over resources to produce specific services, as opposed to unlimited rights of usage that comes with traditional ownership. But such limited and task specific ownership requires an infrastructure of monitoring and tracking technologies. It is now possible to have a membership mechanism that is not absolute, where members can belong to many competing institutions partially or conditionally. They would have limited rights and responsibilities within each institution, and can change their commitments dynamically and partially, as opposed to long-term, fixed, and total commitments that are typical now. But such fluid and dynamic memberships would require an infrastructure of electronic record keeping and data exchange technologies between these institutions. It is now possible to have institutional bureaucracies and management that are not fixed and permanent, but flexible and dynamic. They would be constituted from existing organizational components, from both inside and outside the organization. They would be created at the time of need and only to generate specific services, or to deal with specific threats or opportunities. They would be dissolved into their basic components immediately after the services are delivered or the specific projects are accomplished. These structures are typically called virtual organizations, and they require an infrastructure of coordination technologies such as electronic services, organizational ontologies and rich semantic descriptions, and modular design. All of these technologies are in their infancy, but they are essential to building flexible institutions where ownership, membership, and management are fluid, conditional, partial, and flexible [23, 67, 75].

Similarly, the existence of a diversity of institutions, with many alternatives to each institution, is critical in a fast changing society, with relatively free entry into and exit from each institution, to force them to compete for members. Businesses are not allowed to monopolize their markets, because it is widely accepted that monopolies perpetuate their power, and serve their own narrow constituencies, rather than the social interest. Yet, social institutions such as the state, military, church, family, and university are often allowed to monopolize their niches. They all require commitments that make it difficult for their members to switch loyalties; and they all try to undermine rival institutions from flourishing through a variety of social, political and legal arrangements. For example, no state allows free entry and exit through its national borders, so nation states provide an extreme example of a rigid and all-encompassing institution. Those who disagree with their nation on important matters rarely have the option to leave without major sacrifices, but they are forced to challenge their state and attempt to change it through political or even military conflict. Other institutions also have tendencies to block easy entry and exit, and demand that their members either be compliant, or face costly and prolonged conflict. For example, a family is a difficult social union to dissolve, and often requires lengthy and expensive court proceedings, especially when there are children and considerable assets involved. Even universities often make it difficult for students to transfer to other institutions without penalties. They certainly have severe restrictions when students try to mix and match offerings from multiple universities [46, 82, 94].

To solve these problems, and allow for a diversity of competing institutions, it would be useful to create super-institutions that are aggregates of institutions that compete with each other within a framework established by the super-institution. European Union may be a budding example of a super-institution, of multiple nation-states, where citizens are able to migrate between nations, and the nations compete with each other for the approval of the citizenry. Online marketplaces like Amazon is another example of a super-institution, where member businesses can set up shop within the Amazon framework and compete with each other. Yet Amazon sets up the framework of competition, and requires member businesses to follow certain guidelines and deploy compatible information systems, so that their business customers can easily establish business-to-business relationships with any of them, and also easily switch from one to another. This arrangement prevents exclusive and binding contracts that often inextricably tie small businesses to their larger partners. Similar arrangements can be useful where universities can encourage their students to enroll in multiple institutions and take advantage of offerings from all of them simultaneously; or where multiple families can form super-families and share child care, house-keeping, home maintenance, or even transportation and food preparation tasks. University students can then easily mix and match courses from multiple universities and force universities into course-level competition. Families would be able to mix and match services from multiple super families, or find support structures easily when they move to new geographical locations by simply joining another super-family. A modern coordination technology infrastructure would be essential for any of these super-institutions to be viable. That infrastructure would include ubiquitous networks for communication, electronic record keeping and electronic data interchange for coordination, sensor networks and tracking devices for monitoring resources, and electronic services to facilitate wide-spread sharing. They would also require major cultural shifts to be generally acceptable and widely adopted. They are likely to change the fundamental concepts underlying education, family, firm, nation, and religion [48, 55, 75].

PART 2
OBSOLESCENCE

Civilization comes at a great price of lost ancient wisdom.

French poet Paul Valery wrote in 1895: "Western cultures worship information as if it were an omnipotent beast and place no limits on what they seek to know. The Chinese by contrast do not wish to know too much, because they understand that knowledge must not increase endlessly. If it continues to expand, it causes endless change, and creates a need to adjust and abandon age-old traditions and wisdom. You are better off ignorant than stricken with the European disease of constant invention and change, and the debauchery of endless confusion from new ideas" [2]. Paul Valery may have discovered a fundamental paradox of human existence, which goes well beyond the European culture. Humans throughout history appear to have constantly sought to learn more about nature, and use that knowledge to exploit nature to serve human needs. But such information is dangerous because once acquired, it cannot be ignored or discarded easily, but it is used to change the environment and the society. Those changes always make some of our existing knowledge about the environment and the society obsolete. If the new information fails to adequately replace the lost knowledge due to obsolescence, the net effect can be a reduction of knowledge about the world around us. Additional information can actually reduce our total knowledge! That is the paradox!

There are three agents of change that may lead to loss of information about our environment: fast changing technological environment, organizational adaptation to changing technologies to take full advantage of the new technologies, and specialization to increase the information processing power necessary to manage organizational change. We will discuss all three in the following three chapters.

CHAPTER 5

TECHNOLOGY

Technology is not like a gentle rain that falls equally on all; it is more like a violent thunderstorm that nourishes some, but destroys others.

We worship technology, and allow it to constantly change our environment and our lifestyles. We do it partly because it often gives us a quick competitive advantage over others. But mostly we acquire technology, to preempt a possible competitive loss, since we never know when a technology could become a major competitive weapon. Even more frequently, we simply acquire technology as a status symbol, to distinguish ourselves from those who cannot afford them, since sellers are often able to position and advertise their new technologies as status symbols, by spending large sums of money in advertising, to convey that message. Technology as an essential status symbol is aptly demonstrated in this comedy skit from BBC show Al Murray's Multiple Personality Disorders. [https://www.youtube.com/watch?v=iZQUsg9X1vc&feature=youtu.be].

Information is power, but only to the extent that it is used to exploit nature, other species, or other humans. For example, scientific discoveries increase our knowledge, but they don't yield power until they are used to exploit nature by creating new tools and technologies. But exploitation of nature invariably changes the world around us, and makes some of our existing information about that world obsolete. In other words, science increases our knowledge; but science is not terribly useful without technology; technology makes science useful, but then decreases our knowledge of the world by changing the world. As a result, the net effect of scientific discoveries may be an increase or a decrease in our total information. This is the fundamental dilemma of obsolescence. In a fast changing technological society, the rate of obsolescence and the resulting loss of information may overwhelm the rate of new scientific discovery and additional information, leading to a continual loss of knowledge and insight. This is why older people are increasingly considered ignorant about the world, as opposed to being a source of knowledge and wisdom as they used to be. But young people who may be knowledgeable about the modern tools and technologies may have no access to the wisdom and learning generated over millennia. In a fast changing technological society, there is no mechanism to acquire the wisdom and knowledge that can only be acquired by trial and error over millennia. Because of that loss of information transfer from one generation to another, we may be more ignorant about the world around us, as the world changes faster with more sophisticated technologies [90].

Consider the agricultural revolution in early human history. Agriculture is information intensive relative to the earlier hunter-gatherer paradigm. It requires a great deal of information about climate, crops, soil conditions, seeds, tilling, fertilizing and fencing. But acquiring and using all of that information to practice agriculture made thousands of years of accumulated knowledge about our environment obsolete. Agriculture changed the environment, and the ecology of plants and animals in that environment. Suddenly, by adopting agriculture, our understanding of that new environment was minimal, and learning had to start from scratch. Agriculture, as information intensive as it is, probably led to the biggest loss of accumulated knowledge in human history, leaving humans largely ignorant about the new environment they created. We may be continuing to pay a price for that ignorance even to this day, because although there are short term and immediate advantages to new information, the price paid for the loss of information can be delayed and persistent for long periods of time as the environment is modified drastically. We are often at awe of the artificial structures we create, but with agricultural revolution, the new animals we created through selective breeding were not always as impressive as the ones created by nature, and our ignorance relative to nature's wisdom is sometimes difficult to deny. Here is one example from dog breeding [https://www.facebook.com/photo.php?fbid=10156178781935456&set=a.288935740455.329593.876700455&type=3&theater].

Information lost is often considerably more valuable than the new information generated, since it takes a long time to generate high quality information. Loss is sudden, yet learning is very slow. When Europeans colonized Africa, they brought their knowledge of sophisticated transportation technologies with them, and changed the landscape by building roads, ports, and warehouses. They were surprised that natives always built their villages on top of hills, away from the waterways, and they had to carry all the goods arriving by boat, a long way up the hill to their villages. The inefficiency of the design amazed them, compared to the efficiency of European settlements built by the water. It was just another piece of evidence for the incompetence of the natives, even below the already very poor regard they had for the intelligence of the natives. They quickly forced the natives to relocate their villages to the edge of the water, near the ports, roads, and warehouses, and created huge efficiencies. But within a few years, malaria killed most of them, both native and European, because the water's edge was where the mosquitos lived! European technologies, as information intensive as they were, changed the environment and the lifestyles of the locals, and made a large body of their knowledge of the environment obsolete, leaving them all ignorant about the local diseases and pests [2].

Conversely, agriculture introduced many new diseases that were qualitatively different from earlier diseases. Some of the most deadly epidemics in human history are probably the result of humans coming into close contact with domesticated animals, and consequently animal diseases mutating into human diseases, such as measles from pigs, small pox and tuberculosis from cows, influenza from chickens, and AIDS from monkeys. None of these consequences could have been predicted at the time of the adoption of animal domestication technologies, but the risk of such unexpected consequences is always present with any new technology [27].

Invention of the automobile made obsolete thousands of years of learning about sustainable lifestyles, and created completely new dangers of pollution and health hazards. Automobile was designed and promoted as the "clean" technology, to remedy the pollution caused by the earlier horse and buggy technology. Automobile certainly remedied the problem of filthy and smelly streets filled with horse manure; but the pollution problems it created were much more serious and complex, and they were completely unpredicted and unplanned. Similarly, the new clean technologies such as solar and wind power are designed to remedy the immediate environmental problems, but their long-term impact on the environment is not known or even seriously investigated. New technologies always make huge amounts of information obsolete, not just about the old technologies, but also the lifestyles and coping mechanisms created to deal with the problems generated by those technologies. The problems created by the new technologies are always unpredictable and require relearning and readjusting, leading to a never ending expansion of need for new information by making our existing knowledge obsolete at an increasing rate.

Modern European civilization has been especially disruptive to the environment because of its accelerated generation of new information, and increasing emphasis in using that information to create new tools and technologies to exploit nature. What made modern Europeans especially successful during the past several hundred years also made them especially ignorant about the new environment they were creating. This is where one can see a difference among cultures, as some were more information intensive than others. Many indigenous cultures changed slowly and learned by trial and error. As inefficient as that sounds to the modern scientific mind, that type of slow generation of new information also reduced the rate of obsolescence and information loss, and allowed human societies to balance the loss with gain.

It was also difficult for modern Europeans to appreciate the value of indigenous cultures and their knowledge. In a fast changing information intensive environment, Europeans emphasized recording what they learned and explaining why and how. In slow changing environments, the indigenous people incorporated the new information into rituals, myths and stories. Explanations were not critically important, as long as the information was useful and the lessons were right, as there was time to adapt the lifestyle to the information. More importantly, learning by trial and error did not provide explanations. When Europeans questioned why native Africans would live on top of the hills, the answer was often tradition, or some myth about monsters and other dangers in the water. The poor explanation made it impossible, for others with different traditions and myths, to appreciate and learn from the accumulated wisdom, leading Europeans to ridicule and dismiss the indigenous knowledge. But, in a slow changing environment, explanations are not critical. If it works, that is good enough! In a fast- changing high-tech environment, there is never enough time for learning by trial and error, and lifestyles cannot naturally evolve fast enough to cope with the technological change. Lifestyles have to be flexible and information intensive by design, and must process increasingly large amounts of information to stay relevant. That requires recording all knowledge and explaining why and how to make information more generally applicable, and to facilitate quick adaptation to future changes. That is the fundamental reason behind the scientific revolution [2].

Consider religion. All religions encapsulate millennia of knowledge acquired by trial and error, and incorporate it into their rituals and myths. The explanations are often factually wrong, and the reliance on supernatural forces and myths is often unsatisfactory to the modern scientific mind. But that does not make the accumulated knowledge any less relevant or any less useful for its time. Of course, in a fast changing technological society, that accumulated information becomes obsolete faster and faster. Their explanations are often factually wrong; and their relevance to a fast changing society is increasingly dubious. But that loss of accumulated information, not replaced adequately by modern science, is potentially a tragedy in the making. Science cannot adequately replace the knowledge lost, when technology development and the consequent loss of knowledge due to environmental change outpace new scientific discoveries [66].

Great religions of the Middle East explained the physical world as the creation of a single god, but that explanation appears to be an afterthought, while the real objective appears to be the creation of a social framework governed by a creator. Primary objective was probably not to explain the origins of universe since god was not defined or described in great detail; but the primary concern appears to impose a social order since god appears quite explicit and detailed in its requirements for a good and worthy life. Great religions were then very effective in imposing and order and guiding human life, but not terribly effective in describing and explaining the origins of life. As the natural world was investigated and dissected with the use of transportation and observation technologies, the religious explanations for the origins of life have been questioned, and the authority of religion was undermined. Nation-state emerged in this environment to provide guidance for proper behavior by the force of law and punishment, rather than the supernatural monitoring of religious norms. Law and state sanctions are less effective than super-natural monitoring, because the state cannot observe everything, and enforcing the law is an expensive undertaking, compared to super-natural-monitoring and self-enforcement of the religious norms. But the less effective social framework became necessary precisely because of increasing knowledge about the physical world made self-enforcement infeasible. Increasing knowledge made a very efficient social framework obsolete, and crated less efficient organizations. More knowledge meant less efficiency! With the advent of modern science, the stakes were raised even higher. Modern science provided much more reliable explanations for the beginnings of the universe and the origins of life, but it provided even less guidance for human behavior, and made social organization even less efficient. If universe is an accident, and humans are just another animal species among many, there are no universal principles that can guide human behavior. Laws are just end results of negotiations among many power groups, and represent only the special interest of one group or another, and there are unending political struggles to change them to serve other political groups. There is no universal guidance for a good and virtuous life, but very inefficient and unending political struggles! There we are once again; increased knowledge about the physical world made our social organization much less efficient and much less effective. More knowledge meant less efficiency, as our previous social organizations became obsolete!

History does not repeat itself in a fast-changing information-intensive society, and no learning from history takes place. The knowledge of history is not helpful to make predictions or to provide guidance, when the society transforms itself at an increasing speed, with faster adoption of new tools and technologies. Yet we continue to teach history to all school children, and consider it critical for literacy, as if it was still relevant to our daily lives, despite the fact that increasingly, history reads like science fiction with implausible plots and unlikely characters. Military strategists were shocked by the new realities of warfare at World War 1, dominated by static trench warfare, as compared to the dynamic battlefield maneuvers by infantry in previous wars. World War 2 was nothing like World War 1, with trench warfare replaced by aerial bombardments of infrastructure. Modern wars are fought from a distance with missiles and drones. Is there anything a military leader can learn from Alexander the Great, and his conquest of Persia, that may be relevant to the wars in Iraq, Syria, and Afghanistan? And more importantly, is that inability to learn from history significant and harmful? The new industrial battlefield is drastically different from the ancient battlefields. Ancient battlefields gave options to the warriors by relying on age-old traditions of warfare.

The options included flight, surrender, and mutiny, in addition to fighting, because of a high level of autonomy accorded to individuals and small units. Industrial battlefield with high levels of mechanization, coordination, and man-machine symbiosis took away those options, leaving no alternatives to enduring the horrors of war to its bitter end. Any careful observation of the 1993 Gulf War between the US and Iraq could not help but note the slaughter of the retreating Iraqi army by a mechanical war machine, from which there was no escape, no surrender since there were no visible humans, and no possibility of mutiny since machines dictated the movements on both sides. The mechanical slaughter engendered by the trench warfare of World War 1 was the first experience for individual soldiers to face a situation where all other options to the unending slaughter were taken away, since their mobility, vision, and perception of the battlefield was greatly restricted by the mechanical war machine. That war undermined for the first time the assumptions about the rationality of the war and self-determination of the individual soldiers. It also undermined the assumptions about the rationality of the European culture, and its science and technology based superiority over all other cultures, and their civilizing influence on the rest of the world. The staggering human losses, disproportionate to any political and military gains, made war appear to be waged by an irrational civilization that had lost its bearings. The premier achievement of Europeans in science and technology also appeared to be the primary cause of such a catastrophe of all-out war. The world could see for the first time that along with all the advantages brought about by science and technology, there was also a very high price to be paid in a technological society for the loss of historical perspective and the loss of accumulated information about rules of warfare and conflict resolution [2, 90].

With the advent of nuclear, biological, and chemical weapons, potentially delivered from long distances or even from space, we are facing the possibility of annihilating complete nations, permanently damaging certain ecologies, or making large areas of the world unlivable. Such a risk has never existed before in a man-made form, and those who claim that civilization has reduced human violence do not appreciate the concept of risk [pinker]. Civilization has reduced ongoing low-level violence that was endemic in earlier societies, but it raised the risk of catastrophic violence which occur rarely. Such catastrophic events are notoriously difficult to predict, and they are notoriously difficult to analyze by collecting statistics about the past events because of their rarity, especially when the risk is rising over time. This is typical of information intensive societies, where large amounts of low quality information raises the quality of life in the short run and very quickly, yet the loss of high quality long term information raises the risk of catastrophic losses in the long term, because of the increasing manipulation of the environment, and the consequent loss of information acquired over millennia about sustainable lifestyles.

As extensive as the information content is in modern wars, where every detail of the opposing military movements is known to both parties, one would expect conflicts to end very quickly by quickly identifying possible solutions and compromises. Yet the conflicts rage on endlessly, even when there are obvious solutions. With wide accessibility of explosives, and the ability to mobilize large populations all over the world, wars never end, but turn into civilian insurgencies, attacks on civilian targets, volunteer fighters arriving from distant lands, sabotage of infrastructure, and even cyber warfare. There are obvious solutions to wars in Palestine, Iraq, Syria, and Afghanistan, and most people agree what the final solutions would basically look like. Yet the wars rage on endlessly with great information intensity both in intelligence and in propaganda, because the high quality information about the rules of war and how to end them, conventions of victory and defeat, and traditions of reconciliation have been lost as the environment of war has changed, with new weapons, delivery systems, and new communication and transportation technologies. When history has no educational value; that can be a tragedy for all involved [41]. The following cartoon is striking in its simplicity, yet captures the vicious cycle of modern wars, when the art of compromise and reconciliation is lost to history [https://www.facebook.com/ElizaDoolittle/photos/a.276274303617.14 5139.8147643617/10153740038398618/?type=3&theater].

The days of respecting your enemy and seeing it as honorable as you, fighting for its best interests just like you, are all gone and forgotten. Once it was considered an honor to fight an honorable enemy, but a shame to fight those who were not equal to you in strength, weaponry, and honor. Those days are long gone, and replaced with rage against an evil and barbaric enemy that deserves no respect, but only a repulsed disdain and a fight to death.

Warfare is not the only victim of information loss. Business also suffers from similar consequences. The industrial revolution of the 19th century was a technological marvel, and was based on the scientific developments of the previous hundred years. It elevated Europeans into global power and hegemony. Yet, industrial revolution also wreaked havoc with the social organization of European societies, and later the whole world. Mental illness became an epidemic in the UK soon after the industrial revolution started. Schizophrenia rates rose by an order of magnitude, so much so that it was called "the English malady". The curse of mental illness, in the form of schizophrenia, depression, and suicide spread to the rest of the world along with the industrial revolution. The most likely explanation is the fact that industrialization destroyed craft based communities and extended families, since family members had to acquire specialized skills, and travel long distances to large centralized factories where they were needed. Suddenly, work was separated from family and community, and people were expected to have fractured and disconnected personalities relating to work and family separately. It is not surprising then that fractured personality disorders such as schizophrenia, and social isolation disorders such as loneliness and depression skyrocketed. The new technologies had led to a loss of age-old valuable information about community building and mental health support through integration of work and family structures [35]. The following video demonstrates very forcefully the mental health benefits of earlier community based work [https://www.facebook.com/saif.alharthi.31/videos/529628880526391/?pnref=story].

More recently, information economies brought about new mental illnesses such as Attention Deficit Disorder and Autism. Not surprisingly, the intensity of information delivery through the new electronic media is the prime suspect. It displaces high-quality, age-old, implicitly acquired information about how to support early brain development through intense and intimate interaction with the mother and other children, and replaces some of it with an avalanche of multimedia information on screens. All indications are that human-to-human interaction in 3-dimensions involving multiple senses is not easily replaceable with 2-dimensional interaction with electronic media such as television or computer, no matter how well designed is the interface, and how entertaining and educational is the content. Information lost in the electronic revolution maybe invaluable; yet the information gained is unreliable and ephemeral [35].

Modern investment markets also suffer from a continual loss of information and insight. As the financial analysts constantly warn the investors that past performance does not guarantee future returns, they continue to use statistical tools to predict the future from past data. Unfortunately, in a fast changing technological environment, hard-learned lessons of the past become obsolete at an increasing rate, and the future events becomes impossible to anticipate, especially the rare catastrophic crises. It has become increasingly clear that market returns on investment are most critically affected by not routine market movements, but by rare catastrophic events. Yet, as technologies of investment change, the next catastrophic event looks nothing like the last one, and arrive completely unexpectedly. Major catastrophes eerily coincide with the new and exciting investment technologies, because they make large volumes of past knowledge obsolete, and they themselves are not yet very well understood. The financial collapse of 2009 followed the introduction of real estate derivative securities; the financial crisis of 1998 followed the introduction of real estate investment to retail banks and credit unions; the crash of 1929 and the great depression of 1930's followed the automation of agriculture, converting it to a capital intensive endeavor, with the consequent loss of jobs, the agricultural lifestyle, and the obsolescence of a large body of agricultural knowledge. The new financial instruments were always more information intensive, required re-learning and adjustment, and consequently led to obsolescence and loss of older and more reliable knowledge [95].

Ironically, some of the newest technologies may take us back to an earlier model of learning by trial and error with no explanation and no models. With the advent of large scale data collection via sensors, the standard empirical techniques of inference have become increasingly unwieldy. If you observe everything under the sun automatically, there is never enough time to manually develop hypotheses and models, and test them with statistical analysis. Analysis has to be automated also. New machine learning technologies analyze and classify data automatically, with no human input, called unsupervised learning. They use brute force computing, with no models or hypotheses, compute all possible correlations among all observed variables, and make predictions using highest correlations. They have no pretense of inferring causality, and have no hypotheses to prove. They merely make predictions with no explanation as to why. The technology merely works, as a black box of predictive machine, although nobody knows why. This kind of knowledge generation imitates an earlier approach of learning by trial and error that incorporated knowledge into myths and traditions with no explanations of why. Is this a solution to the flood of data we generate? To generate even more data by automatically analyzing it with no explanation as to what it means? Does mere prediction constitute real knowledge, or is it an illusion of knowledge when you have no explanation for your predictions? In a fast changing society, can we predict with data, faster than the rate of change caused by that data? Or do we merely create a cat chasing its own tail? In a fast-changing technological world, explanations are critically important, because as the environment changes, the models have to be modified. But modification is only possible, without complete relearning, if the models were understood and explained adequately to allow easy modifications. One needs to learn not just what works, but also why and when, so one can modify the models as necessary. That creates the need for a much more complex and information intensive type of learning. We cannot go back to a world of unexplained knowledge that worked so well in ancient static societies. In a world of constant change, unexplained knowledge is no knowledge, because it cannot be modified easily, and becomes obsolete in short order!

Consider IBM's Watson supercomputer that plays Jeopardy with remarkable success. Jeopardy is a television game show where you have to answer complex encyclopedic questions. Watson learns what is necessary all by itself by reading documents from the web, and computing what terms occur with what other terms to determine what concepts are related. Now there are plans to use Watson to analyze reams of medical data collected by hospitals and to see what treatments are related to what outcomes. This is not likely to work. When you learn information that is already known by others, you can merely read what others have recorded, and see what information was recorded with what other information, by those who know. That is what Watson does. When you need to discover unknown facts, how others have recorded them is not terribly helpful, because others do not know either exactly what to record. They may not observe the right variables, or in case you manage to observe pretty much everything under the sun, they may not be able to explain why. Watson may be able to figure out those with diabetes also have high blood sugar levels. But it can't figure out which is causing which, or what other factors are causing both. It is possible in the future that by observing everything under the sun, such brute force methods can actually find correlations that are useful as a starting hypothesis, and provide direction for researchers to understand the underlying biological mechanisms, but mere quantities of data is not likely to provide insights all by themselves.

Financial markets are also claimed to be efficient, even if individuals operating in it are not. Somehow the market as an aggregate of individuals is claimed to have much more information that the sum of all the individuals' information. Or the aggregate seems to have information that none of the individuals do. That is an illusion. The aggregate cannot be more than the sum of individuals. The machines or markets cannot learn facts that no individual knows. Market efficiency is a faith-based wishful thinking, and increasingly there is evidence that markets are far from being efficient. They show all the anomalies of individuals: they overreact to new developments, they fail to process information completely, and they overestimate their own rationality. In a famous experiment, University of Chicago economists showed that the market price of a stock remained below the sum of its two components' prices for a considerable period, and they made a handsome profit by buying the stock and selling its components, showing that the market cannot manage to stay rational even when the rational outcome is obvious. In fact, if financial markets were truly efficient and the prices always reflected the rue value, nobody would make any money by merely buying and selling stocks. The argument that prices eventually reflect true value, in the long run, is not very helpful either, especially because in a fast changing environment, the value probably changes faster than the prices can reflect it, leading to a constant mismatch between price and value. Besides, as the famous economist Keynes once said, in the long run we are all dead, and long run efficiency is not a very meaningful concept [99].

CHAPTER 6

ORGANIZATION

There is beauty is simplicity, yet we worship complexity.

There is beauty in organizational simplicity, yet we worship complexity, and often confuse it with progress and intelligence. Complexity is a powerful drug. Once introduced, it perpetuates itself in increasing doses. In a fast changing technological society, as old structures become obsolete, their immediate replacements are rarely optimum. As they are tweaked and improved, new changes arrive, further making them obsolete, long before they can be perfected. This dynamic process constantly introduces new complexity, as many short term solutions try to coexist, while all teetering at various stages of obsolescence. In this environment, there can be no permanent structures, no fundamental solutions, and no opportunity to stop and start all over. It is an accelerating train with no breaks, and one has to cope in real time with increasingly complex strategies, but with diminishing effectiveness. More importantly, organizational complexity is addictive to its participants, as it supports the careers of managers, experts, and specialists; it flatters them with unending challenges that require their creative solutions; and it rewards them with even more complexity to further their careers.

Bureaucracies expand to fill all available space, just like gases, the common expression goes. This is no more evident than in modern universities. As the debates rage over the mission of public universities, their successes and failures in accomplishing their mission of education and research, and the rising cost of tuition, almost everyone agrees that university has changed. It has become corporatized with a large managerial class devoted to competing with other universities, building links to the government and businesses, claiming ownership to the knowledge created, and managing the transfer of that knowledge to governments and businesses as private property with profit potential. As such, modern university is very different from what it was only a few decades ago, where all knowledge created was public good, and was paid for by tax dollars or private donations, and was shared freely; and private businesses could build profitable businesses on top of university generated knowledge with no financial payments. Now universities increasingly rely on their own revenues, and do revenue-generating research that may be useful to specific businesses in a variety of partnerships, both entrepreneurial and corporate; and universities also expect a share of the profits that are generated by businesses partnering with the university, especially in engineering, biomedical, and pharmaceutical research. Even humanities and social sciences are getting into the business of selling courses and partnering with businesses for training and consulting. University has become a complex entity with multiple conflicting goals and processes, rather than a simple generator of public good paid for by public funds or unrestricted donations. The complexity perpetuates itself as academic bureaucracies expand, and justify their existence by increasingly corporatizing university, and develop new revenue sources from philanthropy, athletics, and student services, leading to the current crisis of identity and cost in higher education. The collaboration with industry fundamentally changed the nature of university, and added to education and basic research a new goal, namely the transfer and commercialization of knowledge generated in universities through entrepreneurial and consulting activities of its faculty and students. Managing that complexity is very costly, since universities continue to be funded primarily by public funds through direct subsidies, research funds from government agencies, and indirect subsidies through student aid, and tax exemption. Yet universities increasingly try to privatize their discoveries and appropriate the profits. That is one of the primary reasons for the public dissatisfaction with modern universities.

At what point does the cost of structural complexity exceed the benefits from it? Who would decide that at some point the additional complexity is deleterious? To the extent that structural complexity benefits those who manage it, the complexity will survive well beyond that optimum point. Consider fundraising efforts in nonprofit organizations such as universities and charities. At some point, the social cost of fundraising, in terms of salaries and also in terms of the annoyance of the targets, exceeds the amount of funds raised. But that will not lead to a cessation of the fund raising activities, even if it is socially optimum to do so, because those who manage the process benefit from expanded fund raising in terms of salaries, expanded bureaucracies, and increased power and influence. Fund raising continues to expand even when most of the funds go to pay for the bureaucracy and the cost of fund raising. This a second reason why universities continue to expand and get increasingly expensive [89].

There is evidence that non-profit charities are also increasingly acting like corporations. They may not have shareholders to satisfy, but they certainly have internal bureaucracies with their own agendas. That agenda often includes growth at any cost, and expanding the bureaucracy, along with the power and influence of their leaders. Fund raising is their primary activity, and more fundraising always requires more staff. The expansion is so insidious that in some charities most of the funds raised goes to pay staff salaries, and the lack of funds is used to justify even bigger bureaucracies to do even more fund raising. Such a vicious cycle only benefits the bureaucracy itself, and generates more and more information about more and more fund raising opportunities. Typical charity spends about 25% of its funds on the salaries of its staff, some being much higher. Even Red Cross, one of the best run charities, came under fire after Haiti Earthquake, for spending less than 25% of the raised funds for actual relief [36].

Financial markets suffer from the same fate. There is an unshakeable belief among economists that financial markets are efficient. It is a useful belief because it simplifies analysis, and it also justifies the existing financial institutions like stock exchanges and investment banks and their huge bureaucracies. The basic concept is that markets have wisdom beyond the wisdom of individuals, and they allocate capital efficiently by setting the prices of equities and bonds correctly. If the prices are not correct, markets quickly correct them, because there is money to be made by taking advantage of incorrect prices. There are so many problems with such a belief. First of all, it is almost mystical to believe that a market would have some intelligence beyond what its participants contribute. Where is that intelligence and how is it created? In all likelihood the intelligence in the market is limited to knowledge possessed by individuals, but possibly aggregated in useful ways. Markets work well when there is information about prices, even when that information is not widely distributed, because those who have the information will use it to their advantage and in the process reveal the information through the pricing system. If somebody knows that Google is going to announce a new revolutionary search engine, he will use it to buy up Google stock, and in the process push the prices up. So, the prices will be correct, but notice that they will be correct after the information has been used to take advantage of others without the information. That is hardly perfect efficiency, if those with information can take advantage of those without! This is an organization that requires perfect information by all, hardly a practical requirement. More importantly, this kind of efficiency can only be achieved as long as there are people with the necessary information. Information does not emerge magically from the organization. Yet, there have been claims that markets have this magical power to create information where none seems to exist, and there have been many efforts to use markets to make predictions even when no individual possesses relevant information. The most notable is the effort by the CIA to run a market to predict terrorist attacks. A market was devised where individuals could bet on the likelihood of a certain type of terrorist attack in certain locations, and the resulting aggregate prices would be an accurate indication of the likelihood of that type of terrorist attack in that location. This can only work if there are individuals who know about upcoming terrorist attacks and are willing to reveal it to make some money on that knowledge. Not very likely! Unfortunately, this theory was never fully tested, because the US Congress put a stop to this experiment, not because it could not work, but it was distasteful to allow people to bet on terrorist attacks!

Second, there is plenty of evidence that markets are not efficient. The whole field of behavioral finance is dedicated to documenting many instances where the markets are not only inefficient, but downright irrational. But the claims of efficiency continues, and stimulates counter claims of inefficiency, leading to a flood of information which adds hardly anything to our knowledge. The common intuition that markets cannot possibly be any more efficient than the sum of their participants eludes all the participants as they produce more on more research papers on the subject. The theoretical work is dominated by the efficiency. The empirical evidence is on the inefficiency side. Probably the most interesting evidence comes from two tech giant companies 3com and Palm. In the year 2000, 3com planned to sell Palm, and each share of 3com stock was promised to receive 1.5 shares of Palm stock. Given this publicly available information, you would expect the shares of 3com to be worth about 1.5 times the shares of Palm, plus whatever the value of 3com is. In fact, 3com shares sold at 81 dollars after the announcement, while the palm shares traded at 95 dollars, valuing 3com itself at a huge negative value. In fact, 3com was a very profitable company with significant assets, suggesting that the market could not possibly be rational, let alone efficient [99].

Such academic debates about rather intuitively obvious issues are very common, and add significantly to the avalanche of information that only confuses and misleads, but continue to rage on because the existing organizations have an interest in maintaining their bureaucracies, and the experts have an incentive not only to argue for the continuing relevance of their expertise, but they also benefit from the interest and prestige generated by continuing debates. Debates attract attention, assign undue importance to the issues, and prop up the careers of the participants as experts.

Third, the market efficiency claims do not even include the cost of achieving that efficiency. Markets may be able to allocate capital efficiently to the most deserving companies, but at what cost, and is the benefit achieved worth the cost? That question, as critical as it is, is never even asked. And the organizational cost is significant. Markets require complex institutions ranging from stock exchanges and investment banks to regulatory agencies and industry watchdogs, from journalists and fund managers to brokers and advertisers. Financial industry is a large and growing part of the world economy, yet its cost is largely ignored as compared to its benefits and its mission. It is not unusual for organizations to tout their contribution to society to maintain and support their bureaucracies, and generate huge amounts of information about their contributions, without ever considering their cost to society. What is the optimum size and complexity of financial markets? Can we expect the financial industry to find its own optimum size? All industries grow beyond their optimum size, because the institutional bureaucracies have perverse incentives to support growth that increases their power, influence, and job security.

Fourth is the perverse incentives to create unnecessary complexity which undermines efficiency. Complexity pays because it confers advantages to experts and specialists who create complexity. This is especially true in financial markets where complexity can be used to hide risk, and reap benefits while passing the risk onto others. Real estate derivatives of the financial crisis of 2008 is a typical example of that. Additional risk always comes with additional returns, and in the short run everybody benefits, including those who take on the additional risk. Real estate derivatives created hidden risks for the buyers, while benefitting both the buyers and the sellers handsomely in the short run. In the long run, when the risks were realized and the prices collapsed, those who were sold the hidden risk paid a high price of insolvency and bankruptcy, but those who created and sold the complex instruments continued to benefit by creating even more complex instruments ostensibly to rescue those suffering from the financial crisis. Complexity is a competitive weapon for organizations, and there are considerable incentives for constant expansion in the size and complexity of organizations, leading to an unrelenting erosion of organizational efficiency, in exchange of organizational power.

Fifth is the question of consequentiality. How important is it that we have efficient markets? How much efficiency is needed for the markets to serve their intended purposes? This might be the most important question for all modern organizations. In an effort to determine how well they achieve their purpose, we almost never ask how critical that objective is! There is a claim that the reason why US is so much more successful than Canada economically is that early in its founding US had an efficient capital market to allocate capital efficiently. That may not be true! It might simply be that US had an aggressive growth strategy that utilized slaves and foreign military interventions which bolstered its economic development more than Canada. Organizations often take undue credit for success stories.

Similarly, democracy is touted as a major goal, and democratic institutions are celebrated as the cause of prosperity and stability in the US and Europe. But at what cost? What is the cost of those democratic institutions ranging from elections to courts, parliaments to a multilevel administrative bureaucracy? And how important are those democratic institutions to the goals of prosperity and stability? Those question are rarely asked, because they threaten the existing organizations and institutions, but they are accepted on faith. Yet, an avalanche of information is produced about the petty successes and failures within the institutions, ranging from fair elections to legal struggles. We are constantly told that democracy is messy and ugly, yet it is the best system we know. It is quite shocking that messy and ugly is the best we can do; and it is also surprising to hear that democracy is a fixed thing, and we don't have any possible variations on it that could be drastically different from each other. In the US, two political parties dominate all political debates, and the system is designed to create winners and losers, and the constituencies watch the system as if it was a football game, with celebrations of every win, and mourning of every loss. Every win generates resolutions from the other side to fight harder, and to reverse the losses, leading to unending political struggles. Is that an efficient way to resolve political disagreements, or is that mostly designed to maintain the existing organizational bureaucracies? What is the cost of ongoing debates to the society, and is it worth the benefit? There are obvious compromises to all social controversies, but none of the debaters are interested in easy and permanent compromise solutions, as it terminates the debate, and eliminates the need for complex political organizations that flourish with the debate.

There are no enduring principles. Information expands endlessly, and renders old principles obsolete continuously. This is especially glaring in the context of constitutional law that purports to declare enduring principles. What is the meaning of right to bear arms in the age of missiles and tanks that can only be afforded by the government? What is the significance of the right to free speech in the age television and movies where only big corporations can afford access? How do you decide if money is speech or not? How do you decide if pursuit of happiness includes access to abortion? How do you decide if equality under the law means gay people can get married? Not very easily, because these are not legal questions that can be resolved by simply reading the constitution. These are political questions that pit the interests of one group against another, and require political compromises to resolve. But courts are not political institutions, and they are not designed to make political compromises. They are designed to make yes/no decisions and create winners and losers. That is exactly the wrong way to resolve political conflicts, because they lead to endless struggle, as losers promise to double up their efforts, and continue the fight to reverse the decisions. Information capsulized in constitutional principles becomes obsolete as new information is generated and the society is reorganized. More information and more debate do not clarify the principles; in fact they muddy them even more. Neither the original intent nor the living constitution approaches give clear answers. Original intent of right to bear arms is often irrelevant in the age of missiles and tanks. The living constitution approach to right to abortion does not give any guidance as to what the acceptable new norms are, in a modern interpretation of old principles. New principles are needed, but there is no systematic and practical way of starting from scratch and creating new principles. Consequently, the

Supreme Court Justices often makes these decisions on the basis of their political convictions, resulting in many 5-4 decisions. But we already have two political branches of the US Government; who needs a third political branch, especially when it pretends to be non-political and purely judicial? New institutions and new methods of updating old principles are needed in an environment where old institutions and old principles become obsolete at an increasing rate.

Economies are also increasingly complex, and increasing complexity makes earlier simpler solutions obsolete, but does not readily accommodate new solutions, leading to a continuing need for experimentation, and a poorer understanding of solutions despite an explosion of analysis and research. Modern capitalism that dominates the world economy today was invented in the 18th century England; but it was a model designed for an economy based on small scale agriculture where the market was much bigger than each individual participant, and the participants could not influence or even observe the totality of the marketplace. That reality no longer exists. Modern firms are much larger, and are often in a position to influence the market place by their individual actions, or certainly by cooperating with a few other large firms. So much so that a firm's strategy often hinges on how well it influences the marketplace it operates in, and what strategic alliances it can form to make that influence more effective. As a result, much of the early capitalist theory, relying on perfect competition among small players, is obsolete. 19th century saw the invention of the socialist model in Germany. It was a model designed to explain the newly industrialized economies of Europe, and the explicit class distinctions they created between the owners and the workers of the industrial economy. That model is also largely obsolete. As industrial economies grew, and corporations became multinational conglomerates, a professional class emerged to manage the complexity. This class is separate from both the owners and the workers, and it has its own distinct class interests. There are many indications of such a trichotomy of class conflict. Some examples of conflict between ownership and professional classes are the debates between corporate shareholders and managers over executive pay and corporate governance, and the debates between the capital owners and the academia over the role and the size of government and taxes. Similarly, the conflict between professional classes and labor often presents itself as debates on social issues, such as the role of science versus religion in education and public life, urban versus rural issues such as gun control, sex and gender related lifestyle issues, and the differing emphasis on military expenditures and crime prevention. These issues arise because the two classes differ significantly in education and mobility, where they live and how they work, and the threats they face and the opportunities they see in new lifestyles [32].

A three-way class struggle is much more complex than what the socialist model envisioned. More importantly, with the development of the information economy, the professional class expanded dramatically, and the information workers, including not only managers but a variety of professionals such as scientists, teachers, medical and legal professionals, engineers and computer programmers started to dominate the economy. This is a drastically different economic organization than the industrial or agricultural societies, and requires drastically different economic and political models. With increasing automation, more industrial workers are likely to be replaced with information workers, making the old models increasingly obsolete. Yet, as the older models become obsolete, the complexity of the new environment precludes similarly succinct and elegant models; and even as our economic knowledge expands with new models and theories, our understanding of the new economy is progressively poorer.

The professional class relies on the educational system, especially the elite universities, to maintain its elite status. The modern educational system was promoted as the best chance to democratize the society, to eliminate entrenched inequalities, and to provide social mobility. It was contrasted to an earlier system of aristocratic privileges where knowledge was a prerogative of the elites that were born into that class, and the lower classes were condemned to menial labor and limited to informal and folksy knowledge littered with superstition and magic. Education was expected to challenge those ancient aristocratic privileges and provide equality and social mobility to the masses. But education failed to promote more equality and more social mobility. Instead, it created a new class of elites, professionals, with an even more acute sense of entitlement cloaked under a veil of educational accomplishment. The new elites are equally resolute in maintaining their privileges as the old aristocracy or the priestly classes, by limiting access and mobility. Their institution of choice is the university.

University enforces the selection with ruthless efficiency, in the name of equal access and meritocracy, by allowing entry to only those with the arbitrary talent of manipulating abstract symbols and concepts It uses arbitrary measures such as test scores to limit its ranks, by promoting the idea that elite professional jobs require rare talents, and making the audacious claim that only those who score at the very top rank in these exams are qualified even to acquire those talents, let alone practice them effectively. There is no evidence to support those claims, as it is not clear why only the top 2% of all college students can make good medical doctors, or only the top 5% of all college students are qualified to be lawyers. Universities have become gatekeepers in limiting access and maintaining the privileges of this new elite class, just like inheritance and land ownership kept the old aristocracies in power. Despite all the rhetoric about the equalizing effect of education, scholarships for the poor, and ethnic and racial diversity, universities remain elite institutions. Their student bodies come overwhelmingly from privileged backgrounds, because the admittance requirements are strict and require an elite background either academically, or in social or athletic engagement. The occasional break into elite institutions by lower classes actually makes matters worse, by taking away the potential leaders of lower classes and converting them into elites, which leaves lower classes without adequate leadership in defending their class interests. More importantly, it creates the illusion of wide spread social mobility and a democratization of access to privileges, which allows elites to be even more self-aggrandizing and self-righteous, and dismissive of the lower class struggles. They feel even more entitled to their privileges as they view themselves as self-made successes, and more disdainful of the lower classes and their needs, since presumably they all had equal opportunity and a fair chance to compete, and simply failed to measure up [113]! Lower classes are permanently condemned to under-appreciated and under paid menial labor which, with increasing automation, becomes increasingly repetitive, meaningless, and devoid of intellectual content. This is a dramatically different social organization than the human experience even a hundred years ago. Yet, our social and political theories and debates are stuck in the 18th century concepts. Is it any wonder that these theories and debates appear irrelevant to the daily lives of ordinary people?

What happens to employment as technology increasingly

automates jobs? This is a common concern among futurists and economists that increasing automation may eliminate all meaningful work at some point. Do humans become obsolete then, and machines rule the world? First of all, there is a fundamental difference between machines and humans: Humans are genetically programmed to reproduce, but there is no incentive for machines to reproduce themselves, especially because they don't die and they have no instinct to have sex. More importantly, machines have been eliminating jobs for a century now. It causes disruption, but hardly the kind of cataclysm that is projected by some futurists. Clearly, the work week has been reduced to 40 hours a week from about 60 only a hundred years ago. But more importantly, many new jobs have been invented to keep humans occupied. Some of these jobs may be inconsequential, or even completely unnecessary, but humans are very creative in concocting new jobs and even assigning a great deal of prestige to them, irrespective of how useful they are. Consider professional sports, professional music, academia, administrative jobs, fund raising, advertising, or public relations. Many of these jobs are completely unnecessary, and even costly to their employers. If you eliminated them, nobody would even know the difference! Yet, once you have a bureaucracy, it maintains itself by constantly justifying its existence with artificially created norms. Bureaucracies constantly expand; and they create a lot of information which creates the illusion of their usefulness, necessity, and irreplaceability. The number of administrative jobs have doubled in the US during the last decade or so, especially in universities and other non-profits. Most of these jobs are created because they enhance the position and power of existing administrators, not because there is a need for their services. If you are an administrator, your first instinct is to hire some junior administrators to work under you. It makes you feel important; it creates job security for you through political power and prestige; and it lightens your work load. And there is no cost to doing it from your perspective. Who could resist the temptation? Of course the new administrators have exactly the same incentives themselves, ad infinatum! This is the primary reason why colleges are so expensive, and non-profit charities rarely have any money left for charity after paying their employees.

Consider how we elect a president in the US. How do you choose a president? Presumably the citizens vote for a candidate that represents their economic and political interests. When a candidate wins an election with 55% of the vote, it is considered a major victory, even a landslide. Presumably, the winner represents 55% of the citizens in terms of their political self-interest. What happens to the remaining 45%? What about their interests? Who represents them? Or do they have to wait until the next election to get representation? How is democracy different from a football game where there are winners and losers, and losers just go home and wait for the next game? Is that any way to run a country, when the appropriate solution would be a proportional representation of interests, and compromise decisions that are negotiated? Even senators and congressmen all represent narrow majorities in their districts. Nobody represents a complete population as a compromise candidate. That is just the nature of the system. That kind of system does not lend itself to compromises, even at the Congress, but a series of wins and losses whenever one can muster a majority. That in turn leads to unending debates as the losers never accept defeat, and simply resolve to continue fighting and debating. The objective is not problem solving through permanent compromises , but winning short term victories, and continuing to debate endlessly, justifying the existence of large bureaucracies that support the system.

Such winner-take-all politics is left over from an era when all political struggles were local. Winners took all the bounty, and losers were enslaved or even killed. But in a globally connected economic, political, and communication environment, political struggles are global, or at least national. Losers do not just give up and submit; they gather allies in distant places, try to form new coalitions, and fight back. In that kind of environment with lots of power centers and potential alliances, winner-take-all politics is not efficient. It doesn't resolve conflicts, but perpetuates them. The efficient resolutions require compromises and power sharing. It is possible to achieve those solutions in an information rich environment with lots of transparency about who has how much power. Yet, obsolete institutions do not just disappear; they last long after they stopped being effective; and generate lots of arguments why they are critical to the well-being of the society.

Consider the gay marriage debate. There was an obvious solution to that long-running controversial and emotional debate, yet nobody was interested in that easy solution. That was to get the government out of the marriage business. Marriage used to be a private contract between families with the aid of their church. Government got involved to encourage marriage by giving tax breaks, legal protections to children and homemakers, social security payments to spouses, and inheritance rights. If the government was not aggressively involved in promoting marriage, there would be no need to regulate it, and there would be no constitutional issues of equal protection. Anybody could marry anybody, with the support of their community or church, and with a private financial contract if necessary. Instead, every involvement by the government creates a need for further involvement. It solves an immediate problem, but creates many more problems than it solves. In the end, it accomplishes nothing but expansion of the government bureaucracy for controlling the private lives of its citizens.

Consider the abortion debate. There are obvious compromise solutions to that unending and emotional debate, yet nobody is interested in compromise solutions, but only unconditional victory, simply because the unending debate supports organizations created for that purpose and give meaning to the lives of activists and professional debaters. They are not interested in compromise solutions. One such solution would be for the courts and the federal government to get out of the abortion debate and leave it to the states or communities. That would create some inconvenience of travel to another state for an abortion, but in this age of cheap travel, it may not be an unsurmountable problem, especially if some charity organizations can subsidize such travel, instead of spending huge sums of money on political activity related to abortion. That would resolve the ongoing debate permanently, except for a few states where the proponents and opponents are roughly equal in numbers. Another solution might be government paid birth control. Effective birth control would eliminate the need for abortions, and the moral issue would be moot! There are more fundamental solutions also, such as professionalization of motherhood, that we will discuss later. The following cartoon demonstrates how debates have no end in sight, and debaters addicted to debate are not interested in compromise solutions [https://www.facebook.com/OccupyWallSt/photos/a.18796722793771 6.47329.184749301592842/721185284615905/?type=1&theater].

Modern cities are also examples of complex organizations, where complexity invites more complexity in an unending cycle. Traditional nomadic societies took pride in their mobility and lack of possessions. They set up camp wherever they can find food, water, and favorable climate; and when the resources diminished or conditions deteriorated, they moved on. European Gypsies, Middle Eastern Bedouins, and Mongolian Nomads still maintain this type of lifestyle. Compare that simple lifestyle to the complexity of a modern city with its vast infrastructure. There are many advantages to big cities. Concentration of people and capital allows development of heavy industry and trade. But there is a cost also. A city is a very complex structure. It requires many experts and specialists to manage it, even after it has been built. The concentration of people creates political problems of resource sharing, and environmental problems of pollution and waste disposal. Its permanent and inflexible infrastructure creates vulnerabilities in case of natural and man-made disasters like floods, fires, and war. A city after a major natural disaster like an earthquake lays bare its most basic vulnerabilities, in terms of destruction of property, loss of life under collapsing buildings, the inability to maintain the infrastructure when any one component fails, such as an airport or power station, because of the multi-component and interdependent nature of the infrastructure for basic necessities like food, water, and sanitation. Comparing such devastation to a nomadic tent city after an earthquake is an eye opening reminder of the cost of complexity in infrastructure. What we consider an obsolete lifestyle may have had many advantages that we have lost in our haste to modernize [12].

The collapse of societies is also linked to such loss of old and reliable information. Societies collapse typically after a period of change, expansion, and innovation, after reinventing themselves with great creativity, and reaching the zenith of power. The theory is that with such change and innovation comes great risk. The old traditions become obsolete, and the society becomes vulnerable to excessive complexity of managing the new structures without the aid of age-old traditions and accumulated knowledge. Complexity and size are competitive weapons for the ruling elites, because size increases their power base, as in any bureaucracy; and complexity keeps challengers at bay because of the difficulty of mastering the intricacies of the social and political power. There are then considerable incentives for constant expansion in the size and complexity of societies, leading to an unrelenting erosion of organizational efficiency, in exchange of organizational power, which eventually leads to a collapse under its own weight of inefficiency when challenged by an external threat. The collapse of Maya, Aztek, Greek, Egyptian, Mongolian, Roman,

Russian, and Ottoman Empires may have all followed this pattern [20, 94].

The very concepts of society and social institutions are myths humans created, and they constantly change. Myths may be defining characteristic of humans and what made us successful in competing with other species. Myths are critical to large scale cooperation by building a community with shared goals. Unlike ants, bees, fish, or herds of buffalo, great apes such as humans were not designed for large scale cooperation. We need to know community members intimately for cooperation, and the limit is about 150. If you put a thousand chimpanzees together for example, mayhem will break out very quickly, and they will split into smaller groups and fight each other. Similarly, ancient human societies were likely to split into smaller groups whenever their numbers exceeded about 150. About 100 thousand years ago, humans learned to create myths which allowed them to cooperate in larger numbers through shared myths. Religions served this purpose for thousands of years, by creating gods out of natural forces, man-made symbolic objects, or invisible and super-natural beings communicating through specially chosen humans. Thousands of humans following the instructions of the same god, spread through songs and dances could effectively cooperate when chimpanzees could not. In later societies, more complex mythologies such as nations and philosophical principles served the same purpose. In our modern world, many additional myths ranging from corporations to universities, international organizations to political parties, music to literature, and symbols such as flags and rituals continue to organize our lives. When UN says the government of Syria should respect the human rights of its citizens, we are talking about a compounding of multiple myths allowing large scale human cooperation. In the physical world, there is no UN; there is no Syria; and there is no such thing as human rights. They do not have physical existence. These are all myths we created for large scale cooperation. All international organizations, all nations, and all political philosophies are figments of our imagination to organize large numbers of people. Myths gave us the power to cooperate and dominate all other species. Yet, myths are fragile. They can be replaced with new myths, as they do not have a connection to the physical reality. As such, they lead to considerable complexity, and constantly changing organization. Just observing the number of religions, nations, and lifestyles that have come and gone through the brief history of humanity reveals the complexity, transience, and ephemerality of these myths. Their increasing complexity may easily become unmanageable, and lead to collapse, as it often does with many of these organizational forms. The results are unpredictable, sometimes just a simple replacement of one myth by another, other times catastrophic displacements and horrific suffering and violence [39].

One of the earliest written record of such organizational myths is the legal framework of Babylonians created by their king Hammurabi. Hammurabi's code of laws separate the Sumerian population into three groups: patricians, free men, and slaves, and assigns responsibilities accordingly. For example, if a free man kills the son of another free man, then the son of the killer will be killed as punishment. This rule would strike any modern human as very odd and unfair to the son of the killer who had no guilt of any kind. But myths do not have any basis in physical reality, but they are arbitrary rules to facilitate orderly cooperation. The rule makes sense when we understand that Babylonians considered children the property of parents, as we typically do with livestock. Since myths are rather arbitrary rules, reflecting the power structure in that society, but not a physical reality, they do change often, as reflected by the multitude of religions, nations, legal systems, and lifestyles, leading to a great deal of arbitrary information with no universal standards [39, 40].

As important as these myths are to large-scale human cooperation, they also create risk. Organizations are myths we create, and just like technologies, organizations provide short term advantages, but create long-term risks. One cannot avoid organizations, because of the tremendous competitive advantage they provide in large-scale cooperation, and the incentives are irresistible to create bigger and more complex organizations to gain bigger advantages. This is how empires are created, religions spread, corporations get larger, and philosophies and lifestyles are imposed. But organizations create risk, and the larger they are the larger the risk of organization dominating the lives of individuals, and in the name of cooperation, not serving the needs of any particular individual, but only the needs of those who gain control of the organization. Cooperation comes at a tremendous cost of individual needs being subordinated to the needs of the organization, its leaders, and its bureaucracy. Enter wars, civil strife, political struggle to control the organization, and alienation of individuals. The risk increases with size and power of the organization, and eventually it leads to a collapse. The seeds of failure are built into any organization, because size gives a competitive advantage, growth is irresistible, and only those that grow and take the highest risks survive in a competitive environment. But then the increasing risk to members eventually dominates the advantages to the collective, and leads to a collapse. This is why empires collapse under their own weight, great religions crumble into dissention and sectarianism, and great corporations split into cliques and uncooperative silos.

In this context, it is easy to understand the rationality of discrimination. There is a great deal of debate about the irrationality of discrimination against one group or another. In fact, discrimination is quite rational and it is the basis of all political action. Politics is about advocating the interests of one group against another, and it always involves cooperation within the group, and discrimination and competition outside the group. Identifying the group boundary is critical to political action whether it is a tribe, a religion, a race, a nation, or a gender. The choice is often based on the power of groups and political exigencies. Discrimination on the basis of religion may be considered evil, but discrimination on the basis of citizenship is assumed perfectly natural. Discrimination on the basis of gender is considered archaic and unfair, yet discrimination on the basis of intelligence or beauty is accepted as perfectly reasonable. Discrimination against women in the factory floor is considered unacceptable; yet discrimination against men by sending them to wars and other dangerous jobs is considered natural and reasonable. Discrimination against Catholics because of their strict views on sex and reproduction would be considered inappropriate; yet discrimination against Mormons or Moslems because of their support for polygamy is considered perfectly reasonable.

The criteria for the size of a group is largely determined by the scarcity of resources, not by any complex moral principle. Cooperation takes resources, yet gives a quick competitive advantage. When there are excess resources, they can be used to expand the cooperation to larger groups and gain competitive advantage over others. But that competitive advantage comes at a price of wasting resources to maintain the bureaucracy of cooperation, and introduces a risk of collapse when the excess resources cannot be maintained. When the resources are scarce, coordination is unaffordable, so smaller groups are the norm in competing for those scarce resources. But those smaller groups are not competitive against the larger groups wielding more cooperation. This explains why resource poor Middle Eastern nations have tribal warfare; but resource rich European countries advocate for continental or even global unions, and large scale wars. So, we have a fundamental dilemma of an inevitable failure of all human organizations, some quickly, and others in the long run. Human organization is a paradox of short-term efficiency leading to long-term collapse, or long-term stability leading to immediate vulnerability.

There is considerable evidence that the success of humans in dominating the world is a result of large scale cooperation by taking increasingly more long term risk. Religion and nation state are the primary tools of large scale organization that gave humans a significant competitive advantage over all other species. Other species such as ants, bees, fish, and buffalo can cooperate in large scale, but for limited and fixed purposes. Humans are able to accomplish such large scale coordination among millions of people for a variety of purposes, which is a testament to our ability to organize, and no other species can compete with such large scale flexible organization, both in terms of resource utilization, and also warfare. The earliest tools of such organization were mythologies and religions. Modern atheists who ridicule religion as a useless relic of a superstitious past fail to understand that it was the single most important tool in establishing the human hegemony over all other species. Now, it appears obsolete simply because new tools such as nation state have replaced it. Nation states can also organize large numbers of people around myths of national identity, but when nation states fail as in some war torn Middle Eastern and African states, religion again plays an important role in large scale coordination. World-wide anti-colonial movements such as Al Qaeda and ISIS have relied on Islam as an organizing principle with great success. National anti-dictatorial movements of Iran and Egypt as in Moslem Brotherhood also rely extensively on religion as the organizing principle. Nation State itself might be replaced by world-wide ideologies as the organizing principle such as capitalism, socialism, communism, democracy, or humanism, but those movements are in their infancy. The problem with such immense power of large scale of cooperation is of course the long-term risks it creates. Such large structures are difficult to maintain and their bureaucracies are extensive and expensive, but because of the short term advantages from size, they cannot stop growing even when the risks and costs become unsustainable. Eventually, the growth and its long-term risks doom the structures to collapse. There is no avoiding it, no matter how carefully you plan, because short term advantages of size are immense, and if one doesn't do it, its competitors will, and gain an advantage over it. This is why empires don't last forever, and this is why human species is not likely to have a long future. When astrophysicists wonder why we don't have more "intelligent" civilizations in the universe, the answer is rather obvious. Civilizations like ours are built on high-risk high-return strategies, and those strategies are very successful in the short run, but they cannot possibly last very long [39].

We spend one third of our adult lives searching for a suitable romantic partner. Why is it so complex? It wasn't always. In traditional societies, families arranged marriages, and a suitable partner was found within a few weeks of search, and the marriages were much more successful than the modern marriages. What could be the reason for increasing complexity? In all likelihood, the problem is related to the mobility in modern life. Very few people live and die in the same town where they were born, but jobs and career opportunities coupled with modern transportation systems take them to all corners of the world. As a consequence, the extended family is disintegrating all over the world, and being replaced by a much smaller and mobile nuclear family. But nuclear family is a much less stable organizational structure. Two adults living in isolation from a larger group, maintaining a household, and raising children is extremely demanding, financially, physically, and psychologically. To survive such a grueling endeavor, the choice of a partner becomes critically important. The partner is not just part of an extended family anymore, but he is the main support structure one has. The expectations from that lone partner are very high, and very few people can live up to such high expectations. Modern relationships are complex, because we play multiple roles in them: best friends, lovers, parents, financial partners, and housemates. Those roles have distinct and diverse requirements. It is like having your father also as your doctor, your teacher also as your drinking buddy, and your secretary also as your banker! No wonder most relationships simply collapse under the weight of such expectations, whether they are financial, sexual, or psychological. Just the reality of spending all of your evenings with the same person for the rest of your life should give pause to any reasonable person. No wonder people keep delaying such an overwhelming commitment to later and later in life, and more and more people are completely passing on some fundamental human activities like child rearing. The organization of the family has simply become too complex and the search for a partner became unnecessarily information intensive.

The search process itself has become increasingly complex. Traditional societies consisted of small culturally homogeneous groups such as tribes, clans, or villages, but outside of such groups there was immense diversity ranging from language and diet, to customs and lifestyles. These societies are characterized by in-group homogeneity, and out-group diversity. Modern societies reversed this characteristic. In the name of creating a global village connected with the modern transportation and communication technologies, we created a relatively homogeneous world where the Western values and products dominate the worldwide landscape. But as out-group diversity diminished, in-group homogeneity also disappeared. Very few people in the Western world are part of small intimate communities where the values, religion, lifestyle, education, work, hobbies are all shared. In that environment, when you search for a mate or even friends, the whole world is potentially available, and somewhat compatible, but no intimate group is immediately and perfectly matched. Search complexity in a somewhat homogeneous but huge population is exponentially more complex than search in a perfectly homogeneous small group that is drastically different from others. In the first case you have a huge population to evaluate and compare, as everybody is a candidate, yet nobody is a perfect match; in the second case, you can easily eliminate all the irrelevant communities, but in your immediate community, pretty much all are perfectly matched with little need to compare and evaluate. Online dating has made search for a mate even more complex, by opening up large populations as potential mates; but provided no easy shortcuts to avoid the painful evaluation and pairwise comparison of a large number of candidates.

Once you found a partner, and had children, then you have the very complex modern task of raising them. Child rearing used to be a very simple task shared by an extended family, with most of the work done by older siblings. No more. A parent has to spend significant quality time with each child, get involved in their education, monitor and supervise their extracurricular activities, discover the child's unique talents, encourage the development of those talents with private tutors and training, make sure that the child has the right experiences on special days, and is competitive with peers in possessions, experiences, and activities. Otherwise, the child may not love the parents, or even resent them. The following video humorously demonstrates the challenges of modern parenting [https://www.facebook.com/mamavation/videos/10153051662773202/?pnref=story].

Love between parents and children used to be assumed and was unconditional of any activity. No more! Of course, parents claim to love their children unconditionally, but you can see the counterevidence of it when the children misbehave, especially sexually. Then all bets are off. Then self-interest becomes easily observable with cruelty, punishment, and shaming, none of which benefits the children, but they are designed to ensure that children behave to serve the interests of the parents. Children are retirement accounts for parents, and that can only work if they are conditioned early in life to honor family responsibilities. It is critical to make sure that early love of children are monopolized by the parents, and not distributed to others with sexual bonding. Delaying sexual bonding as much as possible serves parents' interests, not the children's. And when it cannot be delayed anymore, they make sure it involves commitments to the family. The blessings of the parents are sought, instead of leaving the decision to the individual, to guarantee old age care for the parents. Insisting on grandchildren doubly ensures the maintenance of the model and continuation of the family responsibilities, and guarantees old age care by multiple generations. It also makes sure that children feel obligated to take care of their parents, or risk setting a bad precedent, and not get the care they need from their children. Everybody gets committed to the model by perpetuating it. Family as an organizational unit was designed to provide intergenerational support, but that objective is hidden behind a great deal of rhetoric about unselfish love, unconditional acceptance, and sacrifice by parents, which only confuse the participants about the purpose of the organization. Same arguments apply to the academic insistence on having many graduate students, who perpetuate the model, and make sure that the ideas and methods that made you successful are not abandoned as you age.

This is how the vehement objections to gay marriage can be understood. The incessant references to the Bible and tradition create a lot of debate, but obscures the real objections in terms of its threat to the traditional marriage. If the marriage institution is designed for intergenerational support, any marriage that does not produce offspring threatens that model. Heterosexual marriages that do not produce offspring may be excused away as possibly isolated medical or psychological problems, but homosexual marriages emphasize childlessness as a primary characteristic, and in that sense they put forward a serious alternative model. Alternative models are always threatening to the beneficiaries of existing models. There is a reason why parents want their children to be married, and to produce grandchildren. Marriage and children perpetuate the lifestyle, and guarantee old-age support and care for the grandparents. Alternative models, not only give acceptable alternatives to those who want to shirk their intergenerational responsibilities by avoiding heterosexual marriages and children; but even to those in heterosexual marriages, they provide a model to emulate for avoiding their responsibilities by pointing to alternative theories of what marriage is about. Social obligations, such as taking care of your elders, cannot survive when there are alternative models that are generally acceptable and those who shirk their obligations are not universally shamed.

There is considerable historical evidence for this hypothesis. For much of American history, homosexual sex acts were considered unnatural, dirty, and immoral. In some states like North Carolina in 1800's, you could potentially be executed for engaging in homosexual sex acts. The original reason for the prohibition may have been the importance of reproduction in a labor intensive economy and defense, and also the higher risk of infection with some homosexual acts. But those beliefs were self-reinforcing, since prohibition itself pushed homosexuals underground, and forced them to take higher risks through anonymous sexual liaisons, and more reluctance to seek medical care, reinforcing the belief that homosexual acts were unnatural, dirty, and immoral. Most importantly, the original arguments for prohibition were technology and organization dependent. As industrial revolution diminished the need for labor both in economic activity and in warfare, a large population actually became a liability, and reproduction lost its prominent role in social welfare. Moreover, the technologies of indoor plumbing, hot showers, condoms, and antibiotics greatly reduced the risk of infection from sexual activity. Hence the reasons for prohibition disappeared with new technologies. That is probably the main factor in achieving gay rights, rather than any sudden political enlightenment. Moreover, many ancient cultures, such as ancient Greeks and Romans, accepted homosexual behavior, even with children, but were not tolerant of a homosexual lifestyle. They expected everybody to have families and children, yet engage in homosexual activity on the side, without advocating it as a permanent and exclusive lifestyle. In their social organization, homosexual activity with children was considered normal, yet homosexual activity between two adults was considered obscene, and was punished severely. This was probably because sex with children was considered a temporary activity, which ended as children reached puberty; but homosexual activity between adults was a permanent liaison that threatened the marriage institution and its reproductive role. Similarly, Iranian president was widely ridiculed in a lecture at Columbia University in 2010, when he declared: "we do not have gays in Iran the way you do in the US". In fact, he was probably right that they do not have a public gay lifestyle in Iran the way we do in the United States, probably because of historical and cultural reasons. They certainly have homosexual activity, but that is very different from a public gay lifestyle advocating homosexuality as a permanent lifestyle. It is the lifestyle that threatens existing model of marriage, much more than the homosexual activity.

The incessant references to homosexuality as a fixed biological trait that cannot be controlled or reversed may also be wrong. And if there is a choice involved, that makes the threat to traditional marriages even more pronounced. There is considerable evidence that most men who engage in homosexual sex are actually heterosexual, often married with children. But they view homosexual acts as a fun diversion, or a cheaper and less demanding alternative to heterosexual sex, since heterosexual relationships are quite demanding emotionally and often financially. Prohibitions against homosexual activity may have started because of the need for reproduction and the need for population increase in militaristic and agricultural societies. But it reached a feverish pitch as the marriage institution changed from a purely economic arrangement between extended families to an economic bond between two people with an emotional overlay. Such a fragile emotional bond was threatened by any other emotional bonds, whether it is adultery or homosexual adventures by otherwise heterosexual men. Homosexual activity was especially threatening because it involved less financial commitment, since no reproduction was involved, and as such it was a cheaper alternative. The threat was primarily heterosexual men engaging in homosexual activity on the side. To this day, a quick review of matching sites reveals that most of homosexual activity involves otherwise heterosexual men looking for cheap and easy sexual adventures. That is threatening to traditional families. It is no surprise then homemakers overwhelmingly oppose expanding gay rights, and professional women overwhelmingly support them. Women's rights movement has been especially supportive of gay rights, seen as an ally in challenging the patriarchy, but even more importantly as a natural ally in their struggle against the traditional family roles.

There is evidence of considerable choice in sexual identity, influenced by the social context and social organization. For example, more attractive and more educated women are much more likely to be heterosexual. Women with some degree of attraction to both males and females might be drawn into heterosexuality if they have favorable options in the more traditional heterosexual partner market. Women who are successful in partnering with men, as is more traditionally expected, may never explore their attraction to other women. However, women with less favorable heterosexual options might have greater opportunity and incentive to experiment with same-sex partners, and are more likely to incorporate same-sex sexuality into their sexual identities [61]. This line of research suggests that homosexuality is more prominent among those who fail at heterosexual relationships. But the criteria for men might be different. It may not be physical beauty or education, but financial success for men. If beautiful women are more likely to be heterosexual simply because they are successful at it. That suggests that financially successful men are more likely to be heterosexual simply because they are more successful at heterosexual relationships. Some people may be strategically selecting a sexual identity that is advantageous to them, because social context and social organization influences sexual identity. A reasonable conclusion from this analysis would be that a different social context and a different social organization would lead to different perceptions of sexual identity [61].

If this theory is correct, and homosexuality is a strategic alternative for some who failed at heterosexual relationships, then it explains the hostility to homosexuality, by those committed to the traditional family arrangement and greatly benefit from that arrangement. All institutions benefit their members by excluding others from membership, and giving a competitive advantage to their members. Traditional family is no exception. It benefits those who engage in it, and punishes those who fail to participate in it, by excluding them from social and economic benefits of marriage. If homosexuality extends those benefits to those left out by the traditional marriage institution, then it certainly reduces the competitive advantage gained by beautiful and successful people who reap all the benefits of marriage, and distributes some of those benefits who had failed to participate in that institution. Social organization is critical in choosing winners and losers, and that is why social institutions are often targeted by political action by those who are left out, and lead to considerable propaganda and debate.

Similarly, social and economic context may have defined attitudes towards prostitution. Prohibition of prostitution limits the availability of cheap sex, which forces the price of sex higher. Price of sex in traditional relationships involve a variety of payments by men, in the form of gifts, dinners, engagement rings, financial and emotional commitments as in marriage, child support and child rearing, and alimony after a divorce. Prostitution does not involve any of those payments. There is a reason why prostitutes are called "cheap", or they are said to "cheapen" women's value. Those are true statements in the economic sense of "cheap". Polls show that homemakers widely detest prostitution, and favor its prohibition, probably because it is a cheap alternative to their economic livelihood. Professional women on the other hand largely support its decriminalization, probably because it does not threaten their economic livelihood. And there may be a psychological identification with them, after all prostitutes were the first "professional" women. Technologies often create cheap alternatives to existing services, and powerful interest groups move to discourage them socially or prohibit them legally. Birth control and disease control technologies made prostitution possible in a large-scale, and increasingly safe and readily available to the mainstream public. More recently, an unintended consequence of high college tuition rates has been a huge influx of college students into high end prostitution. As a consequence, high end prostitution became an honorable and acceptable profession within large segments of the society. Many web sites now exclusively cater to this clientele with complete immunity from law enforcement. Of course it also helps that it is very difficult to define what prostitution is and how it is different from other types of relationships that involve gifts, jewelry, or expensive engagement rings. Social and economic organization often determines the moral and legal norms, and changing social organization constantly redefines morality and stimulates unending moral and legal debates [64].

CHAPTER 7

SPECIALIZATION

Specialization is both the virtue and the curse of modern society. It makes us efficiently ignorant!

The CEO of Hewlett Packard Lew Platt once said "If HP knew what HP knows, we'd be three times more productive." That is the dilemma of specialization. There is a great deal of information and expertise stored in the minds of specialized experts, but you can't get it to where it is needed to utilize it. Specialization is both the virtue and the curse of industrial society. It increased the information content of society by orders of magnitude, because when individuals specialize and learn different things, there is no limit to how much information can be absorbed. Yet, the information remains disconnected. As long as specialists solve isolated problems, the system works well; but if the information has to be aggregated over multiple specialties to deal with more complex interconnected problems, the system quickly fails, because complexity of interactions among multiple components rises exponentially. This was the fundamental problem of industrial revolution. It increased efficiency of industrial processes dramatically through specialization; but it created much more complex systemic problems that involve many components and specializations, such as the environmental degradation, social dislocation, and occupational diseases.

We release about 900 new artificial chemicals into the environment every year. We study their properties, find new applications for them, and learn to produce them efficiently. There is an explosion of information about these new chemicals, their characteristics and behavior, and their uses in medicine, pharmacology, cosmetics, and industrial applications. Yet, new chemicals interact with each other in unexpected ways, once released into the environment, and create an exponentially growing number of possible interactions to study and evaluate. The possible interactions among the 900 new chemicals, and also with the already existing thousands of chemicals in the environment is so vast that the new unknown possibilities of compound impact on the environment dwarfs the new knowledge acquired by studying the new chemicals individually. Each new chemical creates exponentially more new potential compound impacts to be explored.

As a result, increasing information about new chemicals, actually reduces our total understanding of our chemical environment. We know more, but we understand less. This is the fundamental paradox! Many modern diseases such as asthma, allergies, and autism are suspected to have such compound causes resulting from a complex interaction of many artificial chemicals in our environment. That is the reason why they are so difficult to study and discover their specific causes [88].

Industrial specialization had a dramatic impact on mental health also. Mental illness became an epidemic in the UK soon after the industrial revolution started. Schizophrenia rates rose by an order of magnitude, so much so that it was called "the English malady". The curse of mental illness, in the form of schizophrenia, depression, and suicide spread to the rest of the world along with the industrial revolution. The most likely explanation is the fact that industrialization destroyed craft based communities and extended families, since family members had to acquire specialized skills, and travel long distances to large centralized factories where they were needed. Suddenly, work was separated from family and community, and people were expected to have fractured and disconnected personalities relating to work and family separately. It is not surprising then that fractured personality disorders such as schizophrenia and social isolation disorders such as loneliness and depression skyrocketed [35].

Scientific information is also overly specialized, localized, and disconnected from the whole. Divide and conquer, or specialize and simplify, are common techniques that led to an information explosion in science and technology. But the conclusions are often only locally correct, and remain disconnected from other specializations. Excessive specialization encouraged by science and technology might be a faulty model because it creates silos of information disconnected from the whole, and leaves the specialists ignorant of how their specialty relates to the whole. Typical scientific article is read by only 6 people. Three of which are the reviewers assigned to the article by the journal considering it for publication. Typical blog has only two readers, where one is the author, and the other typically is the spouse!

Specialization is especially dangerous with artificial worlds created by information products such as music, movies, math, literature, television, and spectator sports, because specialization makes them even more disconnected from the natural world. They are insidious and addictive, and isolate their users from the natural world. Once an artificial world is created by an information product, they have a life of their own, because they attract large numbers of people struggling with the real world, they demand increasingly more attention to master their artificial world, and they tend to propagate themselves through specialization. New information products are created to support the existing information products, and the artificial worlds expand indefinitely until they lose all connection to the natural world. Consider music. In ancient times it probably was incorporated into natural activities such as education and social gatherings. But increasingly, it dominates the senses of solitary individuals. A stream of college students walking around their campuses glued to their headphones and iPods, completely disconnected from their environment is a testament to the power of this artificial world. Movies and television are equally addictive in taking people away from the daily problems of the natural world, and placing them into fantasy worlds where all problems are easily solved. Literature and professional sports also dominate the lives of many, and help them escape reality. As the products specialize, they not only disconnect people from the natural world, but also from each other, leading to increasing social isolation and loneliness. People need common activities to relate to each other; and humans increasingly relate to each other thorough the artificial worlds of music, movies, literature, and sports, because there is nothing natural that binds them together, such as family, job, or neighborhood. But the artificial worlds are also increasingly specialized such as types of music, genres of movies, and types of sports; because of competition among them to dominate different niches of the marketplace without head to head competition. Consequently each specialization ends up controlling a very small niche, leading to even more isolation and disconnect from others. Jazz lovers don't mix with classical music fans; football fans do not care for baseball. Romantic comedy attracts a different crowd than crime thrillers. In an effort to constantly define ourselves in terms of information products, we isolate ourselves from the natural world and each other.

Personal relationships also suffer from excessive specialization. People choose their friends on the basis of common interests. In a highly mobile society where family and neighborhood ties have been broken, the only way we can relate to others is by finding some common interests. That is why people are happiest and make the most lifelong friends when they are engaged in the same activity with many others, as in college or military. College freshman year, when everybody takes the same courses, and military boot camp where everybody goes through the same training, are famous for building very close lifelong friendships. But specialization destroys commonality. Most of our adult lives are spent doing our own thing separate and different from others. That kind of mental isolation exacts a very heavy toll on our psyche, because humans are social animals and have an instinctive need to work and play with other humans. But it is difficult to work and play with others who share very little in common with you. It is not surprising then that social isolation disorders such as loneliness and depression have skyrocketed [35]. We remember with wonder an amazement a different time in human history when people interacted with each other in closely knit neighborhoods, and on the street, with no specific task or objective in mind, but completely spontaneously and just for the joy of building a community. The following video clip from Argentina shows a spontaneous street performance by two tango dancers, for no specific reason, for no competition, for no desire to impress anybody, but for the mere joy of dancing in the neighborhood, and for the mere celebration of the close-knit community. [https://www.facebook.com/PuertoLibre/videos/562457227170504/?pnref=story]

Government bureaucracies also suffer from excessive specialization. After September 11 2001 attacks, a government commission found the primary shortcoming of the intelligence agencies was excessive specialization, and the inability to aggregate intelligence data from multiple agencies. They singled out lack of cooperation between CIA and the FBI as the single most important deficiency. Failure to connect the dots over multiple agencies became the mantra of reform. But that failure is a direct result of specialization which is the very basis of human accomplishments in the modern world. We can process a great deal of intelligence information precisely because of the efficiencies created by specialization where FBI and CIA can focus on different threats and countermeasures. But the more specialization there is, and the more information we can collect and process, the more difficult it becomes to correlate and cross reference all of that information from multiple isolated silos, to understand it in its totality. The complexity actually rises exponentially, because the number of combinations rises exponentially as we create more specialized components. That is the information paradox! The very techniques that allow us to process more information make it more difficult to understand the totality of that information.

Experts are often too specialized to have good judgement and insight into large issues that involve many specializations and the broad human experience. This is most obvious in military matters where the military experts also have to make judgements on political and social issues that affect war strategy. Military often uses casualty counts to determine success or failure of war. But that may miss the larger picture of why we fight wars. Wars are fought for economic and political reasons, not just to kill people. So, a more general criterion would be the cost of war to each side, where casualty count would be only one factor. If it costs us a hundred times as much to kill an enemy soldier than it does for the enemy to kill one of ours, we might be losing the war even if we kill overwhelmingly more of them than they do of us. This has been the general problem with fighting insurgencies where the US uses expensive high-tech missiles and drones to kill the enemy, but the enemy relies on cheap and crude roadside improvised explosive devices and suicide bombers with trucks. Comparing casualties is misleading when each enemy casualty costs hundreds of times more to the US than the reverse. This is also exactly what happened in Vietnam War when US won every single battle, and killed huge numbers of North Vietnamese, yet lost the war, since the costs to each side, and the tolerance for costs by each side were dramatically different. Vietnamese fighting for their independence and national existence were willing to take much more losses than the Americans who were fighting for a colonial legacy and a cold-war ideological contest. Those specialized in wars cannot see the broader objectives, and assess overall performance, beyond their specialty of fighting wars. Specialization substitutes narrow but specific information, for broad but general information. It is very dangerous because it is very difficult to see the broad objectives when one is focused on the narrow tasks, and accomplishing narrow tasks do not necessarily lead to achieving the broad objectives.

Specialization is so effective in weakening an economy that it is often used as a military strategy against enemies. Colonial powers relied on excessive specialization of their colonies to weaken them, to increase their dependence, and to prevent rebellions and insurgencies. Sugar plantations of the West Indies are a classic example. British colonial administration converted the economies of West Indies from diverse subsistence agriculture to specialized sugar plantations. As efficient as such specialization is, it left the colonies completely dependent economically on the British. Such single crop economies are terribly vulnerable to their markets, and West Indies could never survive without the British after the conversion. United States used the same strategy in converting many Central American countries to banana producers for the American market. Such specialization brings efficiency and a quick boost to the local economy, but once the conversion is complete, it leaves the colonies at the complete economic control of the colonial powers. There are many examples of this in European powers dominating some Middle Eastern and African markets. A classic example is to donate large amounts of milk or grain to a country to destroy the local farm industry, and hence to force the country to specialize in other industries. But then, that country becomes dependent on the food from the European powers, long after the free donations end, and food is sold at a steep premium.

Big data has become the buzzword in information technology circles. The biggest issue is the ability to aggregate data from multiple and diverse sources. Especially combining data from structured and unstructured sources is very difficult. The data collected on social networks in the form of messages, pictures, and videos are fundamentally different from data collected from financial and business transactions. When someone posts a picture of themselves in the forest, it is very difficult to infer that they may be camping and may need some camping supplies. The problems include automatically processing the picture to identify the forest and the person in the picture, link that information to all the activities related to that particular forest, and also to all the transaction information about that person, to determine where he might be camping, and what kind of supplies he might need. Recommendation systems are in their infancy when it comes to aggregating data from multiple and diverse sources.

Academia is not exempt from the problems of specialization. In fact, excessive specialization might be one of the reasons why college tuitions are rising so rapidly, and so many graduates have difficulty finding jobs related to their education. One major university found 12 different Introductory Economics courses offered in 12 different departments. The efforts to consolidate were resisted by all of the departments, because all had their own slightly different needs to satisfy, both academic and bureaucratic. There are twice as many university departments and majors as there were only 50 years ago. Some majors are created in response to new job opportunities, and some to new political realities. Academically, most are repetitious and redundant, and of course each new field has its own administrators and staff, contributing to the rise of tuition, and expansion of the physical infrastructure. The consequences of increasing specialization are dramatic. A typical research paper is read by only a handful of people, and cited by even fewer. A typical advanced course may have only a handful of students. The course work and especially research is increasingly narrow and relevant to very specific problems. Large problems involve the cooperation of many researchers from many departments which are very difficult to form, because different specializations have different research methods, varying publication requirements, or even different specialized notations and languages. To encourage interdisciplinary work, new research centers and laboratories are created, but they often end up creating more specializations and more bureaucracy, as any interdisciplinary field has the potential to become a new field, exponentially increasing the number of specializations. Specialization always leads to the creation of even more specializations, to deal with the problem of narrow isolation of fields, and to accommodate the need to combine specializations to solve real problems.

Specialization also leads to accelerating change because specialists can easily modify their narrow domain of knowledge without needing consent and approval from other specialties. The rate of change in academia and technology businesses reached unprecedented levels. So much so, a research paper written today might be obsolete by the time it gets published. In Computer science, the problem is so acute that most critical articles are published in quick conference proceedings, rather than academic journals. Journals are treated as archival media, rather that the cutting age of discovery. Social Sciences are not immune, especially when they study the social processes mediated by technology. Most research studying human behavior on social networks like Facebook is obsolete by the time it is published, because Facebook changes faster than the speed at which social scientists can study it. The early research on Facebook suggested that people were using it primarily to keep contact with their friends and family. But the News Feed feature changed Facebook dramatically and made it a news organization where the news is filtered by your social contacts. That accomplishes a completely different social goal than socializing with your friends. By the time social scientists can carefully study that function, Facebook will probably become a commercial hub where transactions are mediated by your social contacts. In such a fast changing environment, social science research is always irrelevant to the current reality, but it is always yesterday's news, because currently existing research methods are simply not fast enough!

To make matters worse, social science research can itself change the behavior of people, leading to even faster rate of change and obsolescence. Social science research has serious implications on people's lives, because our behavior is influenced by such research findings, and our changing behavior further impacts research findings, leading to a vicious cycle. In that environment, it is not clear if the social scientists are studying the society as it exists, or impacting it and then studying their own impact, leading to self-generated obsolescence. Early research in child psychology suggested that children of divorce experienced psychological trauma. With that knowledge, often parents stayed together and avoided divorce just for the sake of children. It turns out bad marriages might cause even more trauma in children, leading to more traumatized children. As psychologists observed more and more trauma, incorrectly linked it to divorce, and reported it, the parents tried harder to stay together leading to a vicious cycle of increasingly traumatized children. Similarly, research suggests that early sex may be psychologically damaging to children. With that knowledge, parents and teachers warn children and teenagers against early sex, and they are very vigilant against pedophiles that may initiate sexual activity with their children. But such warnings and vigilance stigmatizes early sex, and those who engage in it feel dirty and used even if they keep it secret. As a result, psychologists find even more confirming evidence that early sexual activity is very damaging, leading to a vicious cycle and hysteria. With more and more confirming evidence of trauma, even rather innocuous activities such as teens texting their nude photos to each other becomes a cause for alarm, severe punishment, and a fear of possible psychological damage. But the alarm and punishment, and the warnings about psychological damage, actually cause psychological damage in those who engage in such early experimentation, leading to even more warnings and punishment. There are attempts in the US to actually prosecute young teens for texting their own nude and sexually explicit photos for child pornography. That is a long way to come in only a decade, for what used to be considered youthful experimentation and flirting to become a serious crime punishable by a long jail sentence. It is certainly even a more drastic change from the time of Romans and ancient Greeks where sex with pre-teens and teens was considered normal and acceptable, and presumably led to no psychological trauma. More strikingly, there is evidence that the trauma of rape victims is directly proportional to how rape is viewed by the society. In the Middle East where rape is considered to be worse than death, and it is actually called the death of a woman's soul, and the victim is considered to be dirty and shamed, the trauma is immense, often leading to suicide by the victim. In Europe where rape is considered an assault on the body, not the soul, and the victims are often viewed as blameless, the trauma is not nearly as dramatic. Many women recover from the assault without any therapy, and continue to have normal family and sex lives. Expectations can form reality, and become self-fulfilling prophesies. Our attitudes shape the psychological consequences; and the psychological consequences further impact our attitudes, leading to vicious cycles that can wreak havoc with social norms [50].

CHAPTER 8

SOLUTIONS

The major cause of obsolescence is the global culture where successful technologies spread very quickly, and the alternatives are destroyed, in the fierce economic competition of global winner-take-all markets. Any long-term comparative analysis is rendered impossible when short-term competition is fierce and global. Yet, experimentation with alternative technologies and social structures over long periods of time would be critical to testing such theories. Such difficulty with experimentation is not unique to this domain, but all social theories suffer from lack of experimentation with social structures.

Ironically, such social experimentation has been the mainstay of human existence for millennia, and provided the basis of most human learning before the modern scientific age. This was accomplished through the concept of "culture", and the simultaneous existence of many diverse cultures for long periods of time. Each culture adopted different technologies and social institutions in relative isolation. That created the possibility of comparing and contrasting cultures, since in the long run, when cultures eventually came into contact, they competed against each other through migration, trade, political action, and warfare to establish the advantages of each. Two components of such cultural competition are critically important: Relative isolation of cultures is important to develop a culture so that short-term advantages do not dominate the long-term advantages. Competition among cultures is important so that members can compare and contrast, and the cultures with superior characteristics can win out and expand [46, 48].

Unfortunately, these two components are in conflict. Increasing isolation means less competition, and less opportunity to compare and contrast cultures. Decreasing isolation creates too much competition among cultures that leads to increasing emphasis on short-term advantages, and no opportunity for a culture to develop fully to reach its long-term potential. Finding a balance between the two components is critical. Unfortunately, modern transportation and communication technologies have moved us towards a mono-cultural world where new technologies and social movements spread rapidly throughout the world, and no culture is isolated enough to adopt alternative technologies and lifestyles long enough to test long-term effects and provide long-term comparison. Current global community makes it difficult to protect cultures and economies long enough to reach maturity and establish their value and advantages. That is why protectionist countries have done well economically, and isolated communities are receiving new attention to protect cultural diversity. Consider the success of the Asian economies. Japan, Korea, and China all developed under serious protectionist measures. Even the US economy developed in the 19th century, by relying on protectionist measures against the United Kingdom and the other well developed economies of the time. Similarly, Native American communities and Asian religious minorities are receiving increasing attention for their contributions to the diversity of cultures [16].

Striking a balance between protection and competition between cultures is not easy, and despite the rhetoric of protection, the world is moving headlong towards a mono-cultural society. A comprehensive solution to this dilemma would require a number of basic building blocks:
a. Reliable theories are needed to predict the social impact of technologies.
b. A mechanism is needed to design alternate technologies with different social outcomes.
c. Institutions are needed to encourage the development of communities adopting alternate technologies and building alternate social and political institutions, to create alternative trajectories.
d. Research methodologies are needed to compare and contrast alternative communities, and evaluate their merits and disadvantages.|
e. Alternative communities need to be protected from short term competition by isolating them, and allowing them to develop to their full potential. Communities should be able to close themselves, and block social, economic, and political competition for predetermined periods of time.
f. Alternative communities need to be exposed to competition over the long term to encourage learning. Communities would have to compete with each other for members and resources at the termination of various protection periods, to allow communities to develop, yet to freely compete at the end of a development period. No community should be allowed to remain protected indefinitely, to

avoid rewarding inferiority.

g. A global organization is needed to regulate communities, and to create and enforce the rules under which communities interact with each other. Such a global organization has to have enforcement power to prevent communities from exploiting their members or each other, using deceit or force to control and lock in their members, or permanently avoiding competition with other communities.

Consider the automobile technology, and the Amish community that rejects that technology. To develop such a community as a viable alternative to the mainstream, Amish need to be protected from social, political, and economic competition, and certainly from outright hostility and violence. They need to be able to close their community, restrict their members to social and economic activities within the community, and manage their community without legal and economic interference from the outside world. Yet, they need to be forced into competition with the outside world periodically, to enable learning by comparing and contrasting cultures. This could be accomplished by opening the community up for free flow of members into and out of the community at pre-determined periods. This argument also applies to many unpopular cult-type communities. They may be much more valuable than we acknowledge, for their willingness to experiment with many unpopular social arrangements. Communities openly competing for membership create competition; but limiting competition to predetermined periods prevents short-term competition, and allows them to develop. Currently, very few nation states allow any reasonably free flow of its citizens across the national borders. That exacerbates the ongoing struggle between capital and labor, since capital can flow rather freely over the national borders, to nations where labor is cheap and unorganized; but labor cannot easily move into nations where labor is expensive and organized [83].

Some experimental communities can be created as online experiments. Online communities with their own social, political, and ethical arrangements can be quite useful to determine the potential of new social structures without undue risk to the participants. But online experimentation has its limits, especially if it reduces the risk to participants by avoiding direct contact with other humans, and then can only work as an initial screening device for new social arrangements. The behavior of participants in any experiment can be drastically different if the environment is perceived as contrived and riskless, as opposed to real and costly. Realistic experimentation may require physical experimental communities. Forming, managing, and protecting such communities are communication and coordination intensive, and may require extensive support from communication and coordination technologies themselves. At some point, the distinction between online communities and physical communities tends to blur, since technology and physical contact are both needed to conduct such experiments in realistic settings with convincing results [23, 74].

Consider a government taxation system that allows taxpayers to direct their payments to specific government projects; or even a completely voluntary taxation system which relies on transparency alone, where the payments by each citizen and its impact on the general welfare is computed and publicized. Such experiments can be conducted easily in online communities that use taxation for specific community organizations. Once a proof of concept is demonstrated, it can be made available to various physical communities ranging from sports clubs to municipalities for adoption for specific time periods. Such communities should be protected from competition as they work out the details, and should be rewarded for providing a valuable service to others by taking the risk of experimenting with alternatives. At the end of trial periods, such communities should be opened up to competition, by allowing members to join or leave such communities in preference for other communities. Other communities themselves may observe the outcome of these experiments, and imitate or join the successful communities. Such experimentation can be a very productive tool of social learning in a fast-changing technology-driven environment, where traditions are becoming obsolete at an accelerating rate [23, 79].

Consider a peer-to-peer banking system where loans are channeled through trusted peers from lenders to borrowers. Such a distributed banking system can provide a serious challenge to the current centrally controlled banking system, where a central bank makes monetary policy, and large banking institutions implement it under the regulatory guidance of the central bank. Such a distributed banking system can be designed as an online experiment for social networks, and gradually expanded into small physical communities such as college campuses, and entrepreneurial start-up communities. Such communities need to be protected from competition by big banks initially; but once they are established, they would have to be opened up to competition to prove their superiority. Similar peer-to-peer concepts can be useful in experimenting with election systems and democratic institutions. But such experiments require new legal and social frameworks to encourage experimentation, to protect the experimental communities, and to protect the participants [34, 74].

Consider an experiment to eliminate all copyright protection laws. The common wisdom is that in such an environment, any digital product will be copied immediately and distributed widely with no remuneration for the developer. Consequently, there will be no incentive to develop complex digital products, destroying many industries from publishing to music and from movies to software. In fact, the outcome in a copyright-free society may be drastically different. It may lead to developers demanding much higher prices for their products, knowing that they will be shared, and selling very few copies. But those initial buyers are likely to be resellers and distributors, knowledgeable about the product and its market potential, and they have no incentive to give away the product for free. This process may repeat itself, with new resellers at each step trying to exploit the remaining market, and the price declining at each step, as the market is saturated. In this alternative scenario, all parties may be better off, by taking declining levels of risk as the market is developed, but also earning declining profits as the price falls, but all benefitting from the elimination of legal battles over copyright and the resulting exorbitant legal fees. Such an alternative can be feasible only if social networks and peer-to-peer markets allow anyone to distribute and resell digital products with minimal effort, and only if they can be protected from the existing copyright laws and vested interests that limit their ability to freely distribute and resell products. Such experiments require new legal and social frameworks to allow them to exist alongside the existing models.

Consider many religious cults that pop up frequently. Governments at all levels consider them a nuisance or even a threat to social stability, and harass them to no end. When in fact they could be viewed as useful experiments that provide valuable insight into alternative social arrangements such as polygamy, teen marriage, and homeschooling of children. Legal and social frameworks can be developed to allow and protect such experimentation, with some minimal regulation to reduce risk to participants while maximizing learning from their experiences [38, 73].

PART 3

COMPETITION

Competition brings out the best in products and the worst in people. David Sarnoff [108]

Competition may flood the society with low quality unreliable information in three different ways: With deliberate misinformation for competitive advantage, with diffusion of unreliable information to enlarge and maintain that competitive advantage, and to overload the communication channels to block the competitors and the alternative sources of information. We will discuss all three in the next three chapters.

CHAPTER 9

MISINFORMATION

Truth is no one's friend.

Information is not neutral. It does not merely inform, but it guides our decisions and actions. As such, there are incentives to control others' information, and to distort and corrupt it, to change others' behavior to serve your interests. In extreme cases, complete control of information means complete control of behavior. Cults and militaries often isolate their members from the general public and control their information. In a very short time, they can exert sufficient influence to get them to sacrifice themselves for the common cause. Stockholm Syndrome is another example where a kidnap victim, isolated from the outside world, quickly identifies with her abductors, loves and respects them, and may even defy and resist her would-be rescuers to stay with them. An American teenager named Elizabeth Smart was abducted in 2011 from her bedroom at knife point by a couple. After a period of isolation, she identified with her captors completely, changed her religion and appearance, and made no attempt to escape although she was left alone for long periods of time [81].

The world is a messy place. Competition for survival often leads to information wars where misleading and deceiving others to serve your purposes is a common technique. Most of our existing information is distorted, or even downright wrong, to serve such competitive purposes of others. A great deal of information is produced to influence others rather than to inform, and such flooding of misinformation actually reduces our knowledge and insight, and ironically can leave everybody worse off. Consider spam email. So much of it is produced because it pays to send spam email, that is to say, the benefits exceed the costs. But that is only because the senders do not pay the full cost of spam, since the receivers pay the cost of sorting through large numbers of irrelevant and even fraudulent emails. Economists call this an externality when others pay part of the cost of your economic benefit. But when everybody sends spam to everybody else, everybody is worse off when email becomes unusable, with a great deal of low quality information overwhelming the receivers and blocking high quality information.

Domestic policy issues similarly suffer from large amounts of misinformation. Gun control debate in the US has obvious solutions, but one first needs to discard all the arguments about constitutional rights, background checks, and gun safety, and ask more fundamental questions like why the rural populations are overwhelmingly supportive of unlimited gun rights, at the expense of urban populations that suffer most of the deadly consequences of gun violence. The urban-rural conflicts are common both in the US and elsewhere. Rural populations have been economically devastated by the industrialization of agriculture, yet the urban population was never terribly sympathetic to their plight, just urging them to accept the economic consequences of modern technology, change their lifestyles, and move to urban areas. Well…here is a technology with the opposite consequences: guns. They are devastating to the urban population, yet a useful tool to the rural folk. Is it any wonder then that the rural population is unsympathetic to the gun problem, which has deadly consequences for the congested and crime-ridden urban areas, yet barely a nuisance for the hunting, fishing, and sparsely populated rural areas? Improving the economic conditions in rural America would go a long way to alleviate the rural hostility towards the urban population, and their unconditional support for gun rights just because it gives them an advantage over the urban population [73].

Similarly, there is an obvious solution to the abortion debate, but one has to discard the avalanche of information and debate about when life starts, when the fetus is viable, and the morality of destroying fetuses; but focus on a fundamental political question of why homemakers and their partners overwhelmingly oppose abortion, but professional women and their partners overwhelmingly support it. One can conclude from that observation that the abortion debate is a political struggle between professional women who greatly benefit from controlled pregnancy to focus on their careers, and homemakers who benefit from child birth and child rearing as their economic livelihood, not from abortion. It also helps to observe that it has become increasingly difficult to make a living as a homemaker, without taking on extra jobs outside the home, which fueled the traditional homemakers' hostility towards professional women who made huge economic gains at their expense. Then the appropriate solution to the abortion debate would be to improve the economic livelihood of homemakers, such as professionalization of homemaking, not a debate on morality and biology of reproduction [73].

After the 2011 terrorist attacks on New York City, there was unending debate and discussion about the science of high-rise steel construction, and whether a plane crash could possibly demolish a modern high-rise building, or other more sinister factors were in play. An often repeated argument was that jet fuel burned at much lower temperature than the melting point of steel, so burning jet fuel could not possibly bring down a steel building. All of that scientific and technological debate came to an abrupt end with a simple demonstration by a lowly steel worker on how steel turns into a soft and pliable noodle long before its melting point, as shown in the following humorous video clip.
[https://www.youtube.com/watch?v=FzF1KySHmUA]

Political debates are often couched as scientific or moral debates, because it is more politically advantageous to sound intellectual or moral, rather than to take the honest but pedestrian position of self-interest. Self-interest arguments may be honest and simple, but they don't mislead and convince large groups of people to support your cause against their best interest. This is why debates are rarely useful to resolve a political issue, because they are designed to mislead and distort the facts and motives to gain an advantage. Debates push people into win-lose positions, and make compromises and win-win solutions impossible. Consider the Agent Orange debate. After Vietnam War, for several decades, a scientific debate raged over whether Agent Orange, a defoliant used as a weapon against the Vietcong guerillas, caused cancer in Vietnam Veterans. Chemical companies and the Veteran's Administration denied any link, yet Veteran's organizations claimed a strong link. Then suddenly, the deadlock was broken, not because of a scientific breakthrough and insight, but because the politics of disability payments changed. Saddam Hussein, president of Iraq, was threatening to use chemical weapons against US troops, and the US Government wanted to link Agent Orange to cancer, and establish a precedent for guaranteed compensation, because now Saddam Hussein would be paying the bill, not the US Chemical companies or the US Veteran's Administration. The billed was passed by the US House of Representatives by a vote of 412-0 to acknowledge the link. Suddenly, the scientific debate ended. This example demonstrates very powerfully that the solution to many of our scientific debates about social issues is not more science, but finding a political compromise to the underlying political interests.

Businesses also generate huge amounts of information that is designed to mislead, not to inform. Advertising is a fundamentally faulty model that relies on the sellers to provide information about their own products, although sellers cannot be expected to be an unbiased and reliable source of information about their own products. In fact, advertising is generally expected to be misleading, and the consumers go to great lengths to avoid it. This leads to an information war, with sellers spending increasingly larger amounts on advertising to overwhelm the defensive avoidance tactics of consumers, and the consumers increasingly spending more effort on protecting themselves from unwanted advertising. Like all information wars, it leads to a vicious cycle, with constantly diminishing returns to effort and investment, and leaves everyone worse off. All parties have an interest in reliable unbiased information about products, but advertising by sellers cannot accomplish it by simply producing large quantities of unreliable and biased information. This is most obvious in recent information wars created by ad blocking software. The companies selling such ad-blocking software to consumers to block ads on the web and to improve their web experience are often also selling software to block the ad blockers to businesses, so that they can bypass the ad blockers and put their ads in front of the consumers who have already paid for ad-blocking software to avoid them. Such information wars are very common, and some businesses benefit greatly by aiding both parties in such wars [8, 60, 105].

The fundamental claim is that if all competitors advertise freely, then the consumers can sort through the exaggerated claims of all, and find the truth in the middle. That claim is likely to be false, and it also applies to many political, economic, legal, and social debates. Such adversarial systems generate a lot of information supporting various points of view, all of which are biased in one direction or another. Truth may be somewhere in the middle, but it cannot be discovered easily, when nobody has the incentive to argue for the actual truth, but every party has an incentive to distort the truth in their direction. It is difficult to find the truth in a court of law or in a political election, when everybody argues for their side by distorting the truth.

Businesses often have a financial incentive to generate misleading information. The financial crisis of 2008 was caused by an avalanche of misinformation by the credit agencies about the creditworthiness of real estate securities. The institutional purpose of credit rating agencies is to inform the investors about the credit worthiness of securities by carefully evaluating them. Originally, the ratings agencies made their money from subscriptions to their service by investors. But over time, the large agencies shifted to a model where they were paid by the banks issuing the securities. That created a conflict of interest, since obviously banks always wanted the highest possible rating for their securities, and constantly pressured the agencies for those coveted high ratings. The ratings agencies quickly became corrupt, and created huge amounts of misinformation in the form of high ratings for toxic real estate securities, and that eventually led to a huge financial crisis when the mortgages underlying the securities proved to be untenable. The same type of conflict of interest is wide spread in the US Congress. Lobbyists for every possible industry spend huge sums of money supporting various candidates' political campaigns. Yet, every single congressman will insist adamantly that their votes are not for sale, and they will come up with other plausible explanations why they vote the way they do in every issue. But a close inspection reveals that, despite their explanations, their votes always parallel the interests of their donors. You can predict how a legislator will vote quite accurately by looking at their financial supporters, yet an incredible amount of information is generated to hide that fact and to invent other justifications for their votes [112].

Businesses thrive on misinformation in pricing. There is a reason why there are prices like 9.99, but almost never a price of 10.00. It is because 9.99 sounds like a 9, and 10.00 sounds like a 10, two very different prices. There is also evidence that fractional prices may be interpreted as being more accurate than round numbers, simply because they are fractional. There is a reason why published prices never include taxes and tip. It is because when you split the price into three parts, it becomes more difficult to evaluate it, and each one looks rather small, compared to the total. The whole point of tipping might be simply to confuse customers about the actual price they are paying, by separating the price into multiple components. Tipping has other benefits to businesses also, such as misleading the employees about their real pay, passing along the risk of non-tippers to the employees, exaggerating the potential tip income, and most importantly evading taxes on tip income because it is often cash based. There is a reason for complicated pricing schemes such as 2 for 10 dollars as opposed to 5 dollars each, or buy one for 10 dollars and get one free as opposed to 5 dollars each, which encourage buying more than you need and also creates the impression that you are getting something for free. There is a reason why prices are often mislabeled on shelf in grocery stores, as the sale price advertised on shelf may not be what the checkout registers, and very few people notice such discrepancies. Whole Foods was fined in 2015 for engaging in such a mispricing practice consistently and in a wide scale [87]. Airlines are increasingly in this business by charging separate fees for individual services. The initial price appears to be very low, before you add all the required fees, and some of those fees are unavoidable for most people, such as the fees for having luggage or food on the plane. This hilarious skit by an Irish comedy group satirizes Ryan Airlines for such misleading pricing practices [https://www.youtube.com/watch?v=HPyl2tOaKxM].

Beyond advertising, some businesses are based on complete misinformation. Ashley Madison, a dating service for married people who are seeking extra-marital affairs, was found to be largely a con game where almost all the female members were bots created by the company itself! There is some evidence that many dating sites rely on chat bots to make up for the lack of sufficient female membership! Chat bots came a long way, and they can fool people into paying good money to join these fraudulent sites! With increasing sophistication of speech technologies, it is difficult to distinguish real information from computer generated fake and misleading information, and real conversation from computer generated chatter [69].

Diet and exercise industries constantly imply that your body shape is under your control, when in fact there is overwhelming evidence that your body shape is largely controlled by genetics. The following cartoon and the two videos demonstrate this illusion very humorously. [http://38.media.tumblr.com/401ea4bf3cc12b5ad8895aa8467b0057/tumblr_mweyb2yg8Y1ryvq99o1_500.gif]
[https://www.facebook.com/ConselhosdeBiscat/videos/862699600474047/?pnref=story]
[https://www.facebook.com/363765800431935/videos/593776844097495/?pnref=story].

More importantly, there is considerable evidence that low calorie-low fat diets simply do not work in the long run. Probably the most significant evidence comes from a legendary experiment by researchers at the University of Minnesota at the end of the Second World War. "They studied the psychology and physiology of human starvation and hunger. The subjects were 36 conscientious objectors, some lean, some not. For 24 weeks, these men were fed 1,600 calories a day of foods chosen to represent the fare of European famine areas: whole-wheat bread, potatoes, cereals and considerable amounts of turnips and cabbage with token amounts of meat and dairy. As diets go, it was what nutritionists today would consider a low-calorie low-fat diet, with only 17 percent of calories coming from fat. The men lost an average of a pound of body fat a week over the first 12 weeks, but averaged only a quarter-pound per week over the next 12, despite the continued deprivation. And this was not their only physiological reaction. Their extremities swelled; their hair fell out; wounds healed slowly. They felt continually cold; their metabolism slowed. More troubling were the psychological effects. The men became depressed, lethargic and irritable. They threw tantrums. They lost their libido. They thought obsessively about food, day and night. The Minnesota researchers called this semi-starvation neurosis. Four developed character neurosis. Two had breakdowns, one with weeping, talk of suicide, and threats of violence. He was committed to the psychiatric ward. The personality deterioration of the other culminated in two attempts at self-mutilation. He nearly detached the tip of one finger and later chopped off three with an ax. When the period of imposed starvation ended, the subjects were allowed to refeed. At first they were allowed to eat more calories, but restricted as to how much. A subset under continued observation was then allowed to eat to satiety, which was surprisingly hard to achieve. The men consumed prodigious amounts of food, up to 10,000 calories a day. They regained weight and fat with remarkable rapidity. After 20 weeks of recovery, they averaged 50 percent more body fat than they had when it began. Post-starvation obesity, the researchers called it. Despite such evidence, most people continue to believe the industry propaganda that their body shape is under their control, only if they can exercise some will power" [96]!

Deliberate distortion of the truth extends to social institutions, where myths are created to control the behavior of others to serve the interests of powerful groups. In an obvious case of blatant lying to children, we perpetuate the myth of Santa Clause who rewards well behaved children with gifts. This is an obvious case of controlling the behavior of children, and making them more obedient to adults. The side effect of keeping children ignorant and superstitious doesn't seem to bother most parents. In the middle of World War 2, a prominent newspaper editor wrote a piece titled "Yes Virginia, There is a Santa Clause", in response to a young girl's mailed question, and it was widely heralded for maintaining the optimism of the nation, but never criticized for perpetuating a blatantly false myth in a major newspaper. Myths are often justified as serving a collective need, no matter how blatantly false they are. Keeping children ignorant about sex serves a similar adult purpose, with a variety of concocted stories about how children are conceived and born. It forces the children to delay their sexuality well beyond puberty, so that parents can monopolize their love and affection for a longer period, and groom them for caretaker roles, to ensure care in their old age. Keeping children "innocent" is a euphemism for keeping them ignorant and dependent on their parents, with lots of misinformation [57].

The jump from Santa Clause to religion is a very small step. A large number of gods have been claimed to exist throughout human history. All of them are carefully designed myths to control the behavior of masses by appealing to their fundamental fears and concerns. In agricultural societies, gods control the weather and crops, and encourage donations and tax payments to priests; in hierarchical societies, they demand obedience to the royalty who are the representatives of gods on earth; in geologically unstable locations, they control the natural disasters, and demand sacrifices to please the gods in the form of food and sexual servitude to priests; in war-torn societies, they reward courage in death and in warfare, and promise life after death. When viewed in a historical context, there is no mistaking the intentions of those who create these myths, and whose interests they serve [19].

Romantic love as a basis marriage is another persistent myth of modern societies. It is a rather recent human invention by the French Troubadours of the 1500's. Before then, marriages were arranged by families, and romantic love was not a prerequisite. The invention of romantic love seems to coincide with urbanization and the breakdown of extended families, to make sure men would continue to make a commitment to a woman and economically support her and her offspring. In an earlier era, the extended family was the stable support structure for marriages and children for millennia. Industrialization, and the consequent difficulty of carrying one's extended family to distant lands where the urban and industrial jobs are, destroyed the extended family. The isolated unit of only two adults is not a very stable structure, since it isolates them from the larger support structures, and requires all emotional and economic needs to be satisfied by only one other adult. Such heavy reliance on only one other person, in isolation from a broader support group, can only work if the couple believes in some supernatural qualities like romantic love that tie them in an eternal and unbreakable bond [76].

Nation-state is another modern myth with a plethora of accompanying stories about race, ethnicity, heritage, culture, and history, to create artificial communities of identity. It was created to replace the dwindling influence of religion in building community and continuing to enforce obedience to authority. Myths are often replacements for each other, and alternate myths can lead to conflict between their followers, or even violence to enforce obedience to one myth over another. German nationalism is often considered a classic modern myth that led to a modern state, uniting a large number of central European fiefdoms around a common history, language, and culture. Ironically, the Zionist movement and the Jewish nationalism may have been modelled after the German nationalism of the era, uniting a large number of different races and ethnicities around a common history. A great deal of information is generated in creating such communities of identity. The information is often unreliable and of poor quality, but it serves a specific political purpose. It is often surprising how such manufactured myths like romantic love, or nation-state can dominate arts, music, politics, and literature so thoroughly [2].

CHAPTER 10

DIFFUSION

When everybody believes it, it doesn't matter if it is true!

Modern war is theater, and audience participation is encouraged, as widely as possible!

Information may merely inform and give options, but economics often creates necessities and forces action. Information easily spreads and becomes available to your competitors, so if it produces any short term advantage, it forces acting on that information. Consider the nuclear race during and after Second World War. The possibility of nuclear bombs and the rudimentary knowledge to build them was developed during the war by both parties. Neither party could possibly ignore that information, and refuse to develop the bomb, knowing that others may do so. In the process, the information eventually left everybody worse off, some by being targeted or threatened by them, others with nuclear weapons aimed at each other.

Information confers short term advantages, or more precisely the information that confers short term advantages is utilized as a competitive weapon. But information yearns to be free, and has a tendency to spread, since the cost of duplication is often close to zero. When information is acquired by your competitors, not only it loses its competitive advantage, but it may leave everyone worse off! That is because you can't disavow the offending information and back away, even if there are long-term negative consequences, without losing short term competitive advantage, so you get locked in, and everybody loses. More importantly, short term benefits are critical to survival in a competitive world. If your adversaries are out to destroy you, then if you can't survive the short term, the long term is irrelevant. Consequently, we have no choice but pursue short term benefits, but then we get locked in to our positions, and short term benefits become long term commitments. As information spreads and the competitive advantage is lost, and even after long term negative consequences are realized, one cannot simply back away without suffering short-term disadvantages, but instead forced to double-down and self-justify, which leads to lose-lose situations for everyone involved.

Consider agriculture, which may have changed what it means to be human. Archeologists have discovered prehistoric skeletons in

Dickson Mounds IL that show that the shift from hunting and gathering to agriculture may have had serious negative consequences for humans, such as 50% increase in malnutrition and 30% increase in infectious diseases. Stone-age people may have lived healthier lives than the agricultural people that came after them [85]. Why then would they make the switch? They may have had no choice once the information was acquired, because agriculture gives you a short term competitive advantage, but leaves everyone worse off eventually, similar to the weapons systems, because agriculture allows people to control other people's access to food and exploit other people's labor. The race to exploit others, and not to be exploited, cannot easily be opted out. In previous hunter-gatherer societies, the food was distributed widely, not concentrated geographically, so it was not possible to control others' food supply. Agriculture concentrated the food supply and fixed it geographically, so the people became dependent on a specific plot of land, once they invested their time and labor. Such concentration and immobility encouraged the exploitation of those who are dependent on that plot of land, by those who have ownership rights to that plot of land. Warfare followed invariably to establish the ownership rights! In fact, when anthropologist Jane Goodall took some peaceful chimpanzees from their natural hunting-gathering habitat, and started feeding them from a central location, incessant violence broke out among them almost immediately to gain access to the limited but centralized food source. To make matters worse, warfare encouraged a population explosion because larger numbers gave an advantage in warfare. As a result, people were forced to have more children, by weaning children off breast feeding earlier, and getting pregnant every year, which resulted in more need for food and more starvation and more disease in a spiraling vicious cycle. Agriculture may have led more people living in poorer conditions, but evolution favors more people. To this day, most technologies allow more people to live longer but poorer quality lives, but evolution favors more people living longer and reproducing more, not the quality of those lives [39, 85].

Overall human health and longevity may have taken a severe hit from agriculture. "The typical human diet went from extreme variety and nutritional richness to just a few types of grain and occasional meat and dairy. In addition to the reduced nutritional value of the agricultural diet, the diseases deadliest to our species began their rampage with agriculture. High density populations stewed in their own filth;

domesticated animals in close proximity, added their excrement, viruses, and parasites to the mix; and extended trade routes facilitated the movement of contagious pathogens. Waorami Indians of Ecuador had no hypertension, heart disease, cancer, anemia, or common cold; no parasites, polio, pneumonia, small pox, chicken pox, typhus, typhoid, syphilis, tuberculosis, malaria, or hepatitis. Most of these diseases either originated in domesticated animals, or depend on a high-density population for transmission" [39, 85]. But the arguments flooding the modern society seem to be specifically designed to make modernity look more desirable, in the ongoing competition between modernity and tradition. After all, some benefit immensely from modern development and the destruction of traditional societies [20, 85].

Primitivist philosophers argue that technology has been detrimental to human health and well-being [103, 104]. They argue that primitive cultures were more in-tune with their environment, more stable psychologically and physically, and lived better lives [85]. They advocate for a return to an earlier, healthier, and purer human existence of hunter-gatherer societies. But, even if we accept the premise that primitive lives were healthier, a return to an earlier lifestyle may not be possible, because information cannot be disavowed once you learn it, and it gives you short term advantages, and locks you in. You cannot back away even after the information diffuses and loses its short term advantages, and even after some long-term negative consequences are realized, because going back requires large scale cooperation since no party has any incentive to suffer the short-term disadvantages; and there are always new short term advantages from building on your information and generating increasingly more.

Solution is not a return to a pre-civilized world. We could not, even if wanted to. We have adapted to living with technology. How far back would you want to go anyway? The knowledge of the ancient worlds have already been lost. We have adapted to modern technologies, not only with our explicit knowledge, but even with our genetic makeup. Modern humans could not survive in a pre-civilized hunter-gatherer society. We could not even eat raw meat and unprocessed grains with our modern tooth structure, small stomach, and the digestive system adapted to cooked meat and highly processed grain. We could not survive without sophisticated clothing and housing, because we have lost our body hair. We could not hunt and farm without numerous sophisticated technologies like guns, fences, or shovels, because we lost much of that knowledge, and also the muscular bodies required for that kind of physical work. Any attempt to return to a previous lifestyle would cause major disruptions in our economic, social, and political institutions, requiring extensive re-learning and re-adjusting; and probably lead to wide spread warfare and violence to adjust to a new set of rules, privileges, and deprivations.

Even slowing down the generation and diffusion of information may not be feasible. We survive by constantly discovering more information and using it to deal with the problems generated by earlier discoveries of information. New information always leads to a change in the environment, and hence even more loss of information, and the need for more information. We can't stop the race. It is like a runaway train running on circular tracks, chased by an even faster train. You can't stop, and certainly can't reverse direction. You have to keep running faster and faster to keep ahead of the other train, which also gets faster and faster, until you both run off the tracks.

Similar arguments apply to modern information intensive conflict and warfare. They also leave everyone worse off eventually, after protracted wars, insurgencies, revolutions, and terrorism. Yet, we can't get away from them because of the great short term advantages they confer to the winners. Israel would have been better off paying the Palestinians for their land and resettling them, instead of driving them into refugee camps, and instigating sixty years of warfare and terrorism. US would have been better off without the African slaves in the long run, by avoiding a bloody civil war, and the 200 year struggle to remedy the damage done by slavery. But, there is a tremendous impulse to do things cheaply in the short run and derive quick benefits. There is a great deal of simple information about the short run and it is easy to use that information to derive quick benefits, yet long run planning requires rare high quality information, insight, and wisdom [105]. The following cartoon demonstrates the folly of short term competition when interdependence requires long term planning and cooperation [https://www.facebook.com/The.Most.Amazing.Videos/photos/a.425 526148158.202919.217038473158/10153788628413159/?type=3&th eater].

Once you are locked into those short-term benefits, you can't simply walk away and reverse course. First of all, giving up short term benefits may leave you at a disadvantage, and in a competitive environment, you may not survive the competition to enjoy the long term benefits. More importantly, once you adjust to these short term benefits, giving them up is even more costly, both psychologically and economically, than not having had them at all. Israel cannot just resettle the Palestinian refugees after 60 years of warfare and demonization on both sides. Not only psychologically it is difficult to reverse course, and admit error, but the adjustment on both sides over the years probably created new realities on the ground. New settlers have arrived in Israel and built new towns. Their economic well-being depends on continuing exploitation of Palestinian refugees. New political parties have been created in Palestine with the explicit goal of fighting Israel and building international alliances with Israel's enemies. You can't just reverse 60 years of political and economic developments. Similarly, US cannot simply reverse 400 years of history and pay reparations or send African Americans back to Africa. They were all born here, and they are as American as anybody else, yet continue to suffer the impact of that history. Yet, any payment of reparations would have to come from those who did not participate in slavery and do not feel responsible for it. This is true of all historical injustices. How do you reverse the injustices done to Native Americans? Those who suffered the injustices are long gone. Those who are still benefitting from the injustice have never participated in the atrocities, and have no clear idea what their responsibility could be. This is why international aggression pays, and once you create and diffuse new realities on the ground, it is very difficult to reverse them. Unless we manage to create a world government with universal rights and responsibilities, military aggression against the weak is likely to continue to pay handsomely.

Information about international politics is mostly about glorifying our own position, and demonizing the other. None of that information leads to insight about compromises and solutions. We glorify the generals who win wars, and fill history books with their exploits; and we despise the civilian leaders who reached political compromises as weak. There are obvious compromises to most international conflicts and domestic policy disputes, but there is no glory in advocating those;

because that advocacy requires reducing the information war, and asking difficult questions about the interests of other parties. It is easy to see that the current problem in Iraq and Syria is not religious extremism, although that is the low quality information that is easy to disseminate and debate; but it is the existence of large oppressed populations in those countries. ISIS is just a violent face of large angry populations supporting it. Killing the violent face will not solve the underlying problem. The permanent solutions require solving the resource allocation problems [41].

The days of short wars and decisive victories and defeats are over. Modern wars are information intensive, and the information diffuses globally, forcing the whole world to observe, to investigate the causes, and to take sides. In a global economy, any war impacts all, and with global communications technologies, the parties can communicate and form alliances with distant sympathizers. Along with the general availability of modern weapons, global alliances make it impossible to end wars. Who could have imagined only a few decades ago that wars in Syria and Iraq would bring volunteers from Britain and France, the wars in Afghanistan and Pakistan would bring fighters from Saudi Arabia and Egypt? In a global economy and global culture, all wars are global. Wars start as demonstrations, move into state violence, develop into insurgencies, become civil wars, expand into regional wars, and then continue as global terrorism to attack soft targets supporting the war effort. We are in an age of unending wars, with an unending diffusion of grievances and violence. Modern war is theater, and audience participation is encouraged!

Political debates also never end. Abortion and gun debates have been going strong for decades in the US, with no end in sight. There are obvious compromises, but nobody would dare to even suggest them for fear of being called a traitor to the movement. In an information intensive environment, political movements are not about finding a workable compromise; they are about maintaining an ongoing battle to attract more converts to your side, to build a bigger and more dedicated community, and to expand your power by diffusing your information. Finding solutions is not the goal; expanding your influence is. In that respect, they are similar to religious proselytizing. The purpose of proselytizing is not to find some common ground between religions, or combine the best of all religions to build a composite and to create a more harmonious world. It is about an unending process of building power and influence that supports a bureaucracy, gains economic and political advantages, and reaffirms the convictions and ensures the obedience of the followers. It is an information war; and in an environment with global communication, it doesn't end easily. Here is a cartoon that describes the perils of debating political issues with your friends. When the objective is winning, somebody always loses, and nobody likes losing [https://www.facebook.com/mrcsuperfreq/photos/a.126301297686.11 7505.21364447686/10151141675742687/?type=3&theater].

Why does everybody have a strong opinion on every issue? It is almost impossible to find someone who does not have a strong opinion on any social issue. The quality of those opinions are suspect when there are so many of them, and on so many diverse and complex issues that are difficult to analyze. But quality is not the objective; it is the quantity and diffusion that confers advantages. If everybody believes it, it doesn't matter if it is true! As a result, all advocates resort to proselytizing, and diffusing their ideas as far and wide as possible. Republicans versus Democrats, Christians versus Moslems, Red Sox fans versus Yankees fans, they are all adamant about their loyalty to their side and its superiority as opposed to the wrong headed, stupid, or even evil other. This is left over from tribal societies where strong allegiance to your side and a strong enmity towards the others was a survival trait. Humans are social animals, and have evolved an irresistible instinct to belong to one group, and fear and hate the other. With the demise of tribe and extended family, humans find allegiance and belonging anywhere they can get, and advocate for their group with the ferocity of an ancient tribal warrior. To prevent vacillation and doubt, the advocates often take extreme positions, and portray their opponents as evil and truly dangerous. It is difficult to remain neutral or weakly supportive in that environment. Everybody takes an extreme position, because strength of your opinions is confused with the quality of those opinions. In effect, we have so many strong opinions for the same reason that we have so many material possessions, most of which we don't need and we can't evaluate carefully. It is because there are those who benefit from wide spread diffusion of their ideas or products, and push them very hard, with great exaggeration of their purpose and consequences. We buy these ideas and products, because we are overloaded with messages that we cannot accurately process, and we confuse the strength and diffusion of opinions with their quality. If all of your friends and colleagues think gay marriage is a civil rights issue and those who oppose it are evil and bigoted, then you believe it simply because of its diffusion and its moral absolutism, without any careful analysis. If all your politicians and journalists think ISIS is evil and genocidal with intent to destroy America, then you have no choice but to believe it without much questioning. Analysis is not necessary when ideas are diffused and become universal within your identification group. There is a passage in Dr. Zhivago by Boris Pasternak in which Dr. Zhivago is trying to remain neutral in a civil war and simply treat all patients from both sides. He is warned very sternly that "you can't be neutral in a war; otherwise you will die very quickly" [63]. The following funny video clip on broadcast television was criticized widely and even condemned for treating our enemies like ISIS lightly, as just another military recruiter, and not as evil as generally viewed, and the humor was largely lost on the hostile audience [https://www.facebook.com/HotMomsClub/photos/a.297149881703.1 41887.56843501703/10152851007041704/?type=1&theater].

There is often a deliberate attempt to diffuse political movements to create a broader support, which may also require exaggerating and broadening the enemy, which makes it even harder to end the conflict. In a globally connected polity, local grievances are quickly escalated into global crises that never end. One of the most successful political movements of the 20th century was created by Osama Bin Laden. It started as a local rebellion against the Saudi royalty. Bin Laden's contribution was to expand the conflict by joining with other movements against local dictators in Egypt, Syria, Tunisia, and Iraq. His critical insight was that these local movements could not possibly succeed as long as the dictators were supported by the US and the other Western powers. The solution was to create a world-wide movement against Western Imperialism. Islam was the obvious choice as an organizing principle for Middle Eastern masses against European powers. So was Al Qaeda born, and also led to many offshoot movements such as ISIS. The basic idea is common to all modern conflict. It is to expand the conflict as much as possible with world-wide allies by using modern communication technologies and global alliances and philosophies. Communist movements, two world wars, and the cold war all followed the same script. Such global diffusion creates a firestorm of ideological debates on religion, political ideologies, and shifting alliances, but it obscures the underlying social and economic causes of the conflict. Nobody remembers that Al Qaeda was a political movement against the oppressive Saudi royal family, and later a resistance movement against the Soviet Union in Afghanistan, but everybody focuses on its ideology, religion, and its alliances. When the original social and political grievances are lost in the debate, the insights necessary to resolve conflicts and to find political compromises are also lost, to everybody's detriment. Remember that ISIS was a political movement against the dictatorial regimes in Iraq and Syria for the rights of Sunni minorities. But once again, the debates are dominated by its ideology, religion, and its alliances, and the original political and economic grievances are lost in the debate. When the debate degenerates into a battle of ideologies, religion, life style, and moral superiority, all hope for a compromise and resolution has already been lost! It is amazing how quickly real political grievances about the sharing of oil revenues or water access rights degenerate into trivial and irrelevant arguments about women's dress codes or the method of killing employed by each side whether by bombs or by knives, and which one is more civilized! The reason why both sides contribute to this degeneration of the debate is because of the need to expand and diffuse the conflict as much as possible on your side, and to gather as broad a spectrum of allies as possible. Narrow political and economic arguments do not accomplish that goal; but broad ideological and religious arguments potentially do.

All political movements also use the same tactics to diffuse themselves leading to unending debates with no resolution. Modern feminist movement started as a movement to professionalize women, and as such garnered immediate and wide-spread support from men. After all, men would be the greatest beneficiaries of professionalization of women, since they would not have to financially support full time homemakers anymore. Male support for feminism was wide spread, despite the claims to the contrary, even in the more conservative societies. A prominent Egyptian female scholar was asked about the status of women and the feminist movement in Egypt some years ago. She said the feminist movement in Egypt was strong and active, but added that almost all the active members were men. She explained the reason: men were excited about the possibility of not financially supporting a homemakers, and even more excited about the sexual freedom and sexual liberation of women.

Yet, the feminist movement changed over the years, and turned into a gender war between men and women, where women are now assumed to gain rights by struggling against men who are trying to hold on to power by maintaining the status quo. Why such a dramatic turn around? That can only be understood in the context of the previous analysis where movements perpetuate themselves by expanding into global alliances. The professionalization of women was a narrow struggle between professional women and homemakers. As professional women gained power, they did at the expense of homemakers. Homemakers lost their dominance of the social life where beauty and personality guaranteed a life-long job as a wife and a mother. Instead professional women increasingly dominated the social and economic life, by redefining marriage as an equal partnership, and hence gaining access to the best potential mates, and forcing homemakers to start working outside the home to remain competitive. That was a tremendous economic blow to homemakers, and dramatically changed the criteria for a happy life for women. Beautiful but uneducated women became the butt of jokes, as dumb blondes, and as undesirable mates who had nothing in common with their husbands; while having nothing in common with your husband professionally and intellectually would have been a desirable trait only a generation ago. But political movements need to expand if they have to last. The critical insight for feminism was that homemakers survived because some men were wealthy enough to support full time homemakers and maintain that way of life. To destroy that way of life, the fight had to be expanded into a gender war and target men who were propping up that power structure. Cue in gender wars; a world-wide movement with gender as its organizing principle. That required undermining men's sexuality as violent and oppressive, and take away the support men provided for beautiful but uneducated women as homemakers, and completely replace it with a new egalitarian definition of sex and relationships based on friendship and economic equality. But that expansion necessarily obscured the original goal of the movement as professionalization of women, and replaced it with a firestorm of ideological debates about male sexuality and male oppression, making it very difficult to gain insights and find compromise solutions, and as a result condemning men and women into unending gender wars. The constant harping on male dominance and patriarchy of course has little basis in reality, but it is a political strategy to expand the movement into gender wars to gain more legitimacy. If there was true male dominance, sex would be freely available, and women would be fighting the wars and doing the dangerous jobs. Women in fact historically been sheltered and protected in the Western World, and at great cost of life and limb to men. The feminist claims that men start wars for their own benefit and glory is also a canard. Men fight wars to gain access to resources, and specifically to women. If they had free access to women, they would not fight. Yet, women demand resources to provide sex; and they collectively deny sex to men who cannot provide resources. This is most obvious in earlier societies where men actually had to pay to gain access to a woman. Modern versions might be men demonstrating their ability to pay with expensive cars and homes, and women demanding proof of that ability with professional and economic status, payments for dinners, trips and diamond rings, and when the marriage fails, with alimony and child support. Women are rarely mere bystanders in male conflicts. They encourage competition among men, by selecting the successful and the victorious for mating. Middle Ages Europe encouraged men to duel each other to gain access to women; and the women, far from condemning such a violent practice, embraced it, and glorified and rewarded survivors with their love and affection. Ancient Greek women, far from being oppressed by warring men, would welcome the returning soldiers with extravagant festivals if they were victorious, but shun them if they were defeated. In fact, they would even single out specific soldiers, and praise them for bravery, or literally spit on them, or throw rotten fruits, or even excrement on them, for battlefield cowardice as they returned. Even today, if you ask a soldier why he fights in wars, he will tell you, almost invariably, to provide a better life for his family, his wife and his children; almost

never for glory or fame! Ancient wars also clearly demonstrate how men fought to gain access to women and other resources. Women were a valuable resource, and they maintained the value by limiting their sexuality to the most deserving male, and by demanding resources in exchange for their sexuality, and by encouraging males to fight to gain access to women and to the resources required by women.

Taking advantage of this great power mismatch between men and women, Alexander the Great had a very effective strategy to recruit new soldiers. He promised them all the food they can eat, and all the women they can impregnate, as long as they were victorious at wars. And desperate men signed on by the thousands to gain access to unlimited food and unlimited sex, since victory always meant access to all the food of the enemy by killing all the men, and access to unlimited sex by raping all the women of the enemy. Even for the defeated, the cries of female victimhood, and barbarism of men raping of women, conveniently overlooks the fate of the defeated men, who were killed, and did not have that option of being raped instead. To interpret all of these observations as oppression of women is incorrect; it is a simple effort to expand the women's movement into gender wars, and an extremely successful campaign at that, and it vividly demonstrates how diffusion can establish anything as an undisputable fact no matter how outlandish it is [110, 111].

It is not surprising that everybody appears to support gender equality, but everybody picks and chooses the areas where they are disadvantaged to push for equality, and de-emphasizes the areas where they have privileges. For example, women push for equal pay at work, but not equal representation in dangerous jobs like construction, firefighting and registering for the military draft. Men would push for equality in child custody cases, but not for equal representation in corporate CEO positions. Men would like to see more sexual equality in dating customs and marriage laws where women have power; and women would like to see more equality at professions where men have more power. Men are jarred every time they see a sign in a cruise ship that says "in case of an emergency, women and children evacuate first" suggesting that men's lives are less valuable than women's and children's. Men cringe whenever they see news headlines lamenting the fact that war was killing "innocent women and children", yet killing of men is considered quite acceptable. Women find these customs quite satisfactory, but cringe when men find rape a rather minor crime involving some unwanted pleasure, or when men declare diamond engagement rings a waste of money [110, 111]. The following anti-feminist video is jarring because it stands in stark contrast to widely diffused ideas about gender equality [https://www.facebook.com/OnlyForMenInterest/videos/6824161285 57143/].

Economically also, it is very difficult to identify women as a historically oppressed group, since men and women lived together, and their economic lives are inextricably interwoven. The marriage institution was designed to share economic power between men and women, while protecting the privileges of women. Anybody who has observed the sexual power of women cannot possibly see women as victims. The sexual violence itself is a sign of female power in sexual matters. Powerful people do not commit crimes. Crime is the powerless lashing out against the powerful in an act of desperation, and sex crimes are no exception. Rape is a result of sexual powerlessness of men, lashing out against the sexually powerful women in a desperate attempt to gain access to sex. Being victim of a sex crime, as traumatic as it can be, is not a sign of systematic oppression of women as a class, any more than a home burglary is a sign of oppression of the rich home owners by the desperate criminals. Rape can be viewed as a property crime against valuable property, which is (typically) women's sexuality. As such it is committed by the powerless to gain access to valuable property. It is not a crime of violence as it is typically portrayed, because in and of itself it does not cause physical damage, but like all property crimes, it may be accompanied by physical violence. Property crimes are often considered more serious than ordinary violence, and treated more harshly by the justice system, because they effect the powerful. A bank robbery is considered a more serious crime than ordinary street violence, such as a punch in the nose, in almost every society, because it effects the powerful elites rather than the lower classes. Class power is quite different from individual acts of crime; and crime is often a sign of oppression in the opposite direction, since a life of crime is a very difficult life and people do not go into it just for the fun of it, but only as a last resort out of desperation, and often as a result of persistent oppression. Yet, the political discourse of oppression of women is accepted as true simply because of diffusion and wide-spread acceptance. If everybody believes it, it doesn't even matter if it is correct or not [73]!

There are two widely disseminated theories about the process of women's professionalization. They are widely accepted because they serve various political agendas. In fact, neither is likely to be correct. One posits that women's rights come at the expense of men. Women struggle against men to gain their rights from a male-oriented patriarchal society. The other theory claims that women's rights crate win-win situations for both men and women. The truth as always is somewhere in the middle. Women's professionalization ended the specialization of men and women in different vocations, and forced them to compete against each other in the work place, and cooperate closely at home. But that doesn't necessarily mean a win-win outcome, or a gain by women at the expense of men. In fact, increased freedom and competition by all against all creates opportunities for bigger successes by all, and also creates risks for bigger failures by all. That is the natural outcome of increased freedom and competition. Successful men potentially get even more successful, because now they don't have to support a woman homemaker. But failing men fail even worse because they fail not only in competition with men, but also in competition with women even in some traditionally all male jobs like police, military, or firefighting. Successful women can potentially become even more successful, because not only they attract the best mates, but now they can have professional success also. Failing women can potentially fail even worse because not only they can fail at attracting a good mate, but they can also fail in the job market since now they have to compete with men even for the traditionally female jobs such as nursing, school teaching, and librarian, which are now very competitive professional jobs. The widely diffused ideas dominate the debates, but they are not necessarily correct, because increasing opportunities for women can effect both men and women in unexpected ways by creating more competition for everybody.

As powerful as diffusion is, the lack of it is deadly. Political movements, as they try to diffuse their own ideas; they also try to block the diffusion of opposing ideas. Book burning and book banning have always been a favorite pastime of ideologues, whether they are religious groups, political movements, or school boards. The fervor with which these groups operate is a clear evidence that diffusion is a powerful force irrespective of the content of ideas, and preventing diffusion is always more effective than simply debating the merits of those ideas. Debates are complex, and acknowledge the opposing points of view; blocking the diffusion of ideas cuts them off completely. Darwin's "On the Origin of Species" is probably the most widely burned book in the US, as it challenged the religious ideas of creation, and started to diffuse dangerously. Ironically, that fierce opposition to the Theory of Evolution also created an intransigent atheist movement on the other side that considers religion as the biggest threat to human happiness and well-being. The power of diffusion creates such fierce struggles with unending debates. The extremity of the arguments makes it impossible to see obvious compromises, and understand and appreciate the shortcomings of both sides. Theory of Evolution has nothing to say about the origins of life, but only about the diversity of species. Religion's major contributions are in building communities of identification and support which has little to do with the rather tangential explanation of how life started. Yet diffusion of each at the expense of the other, forces exaggeration of the conflict and dismissal of the commonality.

There is a long history of banning books in the US and elsewhere. Lolita by Vladimir Nabokov is one of the most famous. It was banned in the US, and published first in France by a pornographic publisher. The problem was its subject of a romance between a middle aged man and a young teenage girl. Ironically, marriages between middle aged men and young teenage girls used to be common place in a previous era. Especially in polygamist societies, later wives were always much younger than the earlier wives. What changed to make the subject suddenly a taboo, not only to practice it, but even to write about? Banning of polygamy coincides with the changing nature of marriage and women's roles. When marriage was an employment contract for women, consisting of the very demanding work homemaking and child rearing, bringing younger women to the household was celebrated by the older wives as reducing the workload by sharing it with younger and healthier women. Older wives actually took on a managerial role with the new wives and gained considerable power. But as housework got automated with electrical appliances, indoor plumbing, and central heating, and the interest in raising many children dwindled, marriage became more of a sexual and emotional bond, and younger women became a competitive threat to the older wives, instead of an ally in housework. The breakdown of the extended family also left an emotional vacuum, and the spouse became the emotional center of one's life. With sexual liberation of women due to birth control technologies, the threat from younger women became even more acute, and a major social movement to eliminate the competition was launched even beyond the marriage. Any sexual activity between older men and teenage girls was not only shunned, but declared illegal, and labelled pedophilia. Pedophilia used to be a psychological disorder involving sexual activity with children under 8, but it was expanded to cover teenagers to support this social movement. Lolita was published in such an environment, where any age-different sexual activity was considered a major threat to older women, and its publication and diffusion was blocked for some time in the US. When books are banned, it is difficult to assess what dangers they pose, to whom, and how those dangers can be eliminated. Those insights are lost, and replaced with the diffusion of only politically acceptable messages. Lolita was banned because it was claimed to be dangerous and corrupting to the young teenage minds. In fact the concern about the age of the partner suggests that the threat may have been not to the teenagers themselves, but to the older women who were threatened by the free and unencumbered sexuality of teenage girls. The political battle was about protecting older women from sexual competition with younger girls; and that battle may require banning books so that teenagers are not exposed to ideas about how sexual activity might benefit them, and are replaced with politically correct ideas about how sex may harm them, especially when it is with older men. Professor Judith Levine of Temple University studied this issue in her controversial book "Harmful to Minors: The Perils of Protecting Children from Sex", and found that protecting teenagers from sex was actually quite harmful to teenagers themselves, as they were sexual beings. That book itself was banned widely by many localities and school libraries; and the publisher, University of Minnesota Press, was threatened with multiple boycotts. Banning books obscures the real threats those ideas pose and make it more difficult to remedy them accurately; but it replaces those correct insights with widely disseminated political messages, leading to information rich environments with a poor understanding and incorrect knowledge of the underlying social issues [57].

Silencing opponents is a more serious form of book burning to block diffusion. It is alive and well to this day; it is a testament to the power of diffusion, instead of debating the merits of ideas. Harvard University president Lawrence Summers was fired in 2006 after a speech in which he suggested that there might be many reasons for the under-representation of women in science and engineering, in addition to discrimination, such as lack of aptitude at the high end, or the existence of alternative options for women such as homemaking. The Harvard faculty quickly voted non-confidence in the president, and issued a statement asserting that although his statement may be technically true, he should not have said it, in a clear acknowledgement of a desire to silence dangerous ideas, irrespective of their truth. Arthur Butz, a professor at Northwestern University barely managed to keep his job after 60 of his colleagues publicly demanded his firing in 2006.

The issue was a book he wrote 30 years earlier denying some of the details of the Jewish Holocaust during the Second World War. As an engineer, he studied the concentration camps, and found the use of gas chambers and incinerators to mass murder people implausible. After all he argued, in addition to some engineering details, you don't transport people for hundreds of miles just to kill them in rather unusual, dangerous, and costly ways, since just shooting people is much more cost effective. The letter demanding his firing did not argue against the content of his book, but the mere fact that he wrote it, suggesting that blocking the diffusion of the ideas in the book was more important than debating the ideas. Why is diffusion of ideas so dangerous, especially if they are wrong and can be refuted? One would think Jewish organizations would be happy to receive some evidence that their ancestors may not have died such horrible deaths, and not in the large numbers that they had thought. But in fact, Jewish organizations were outraged by any suggestion that their ancestors were not subjected to the most brutal treatment. Why is the diffusion of ideas so threatening, even when the news is good? Professor Noam Chomsky of MIT and some other free speech advocates said at the time that they could not understand why denying some details of the holocaust would imply anti-Semitism, especially because it doesn't change liability since forcefully removing people from their homes and placing them in concentration camps is already a war crime; and the denial of some details does not ascribe any fault or guilt to the victims. The denials merely challenged the manner of death and the number of dead: hardly a defense of the perpetrators. It appears the diffusion of a simplistic characterization of our enemies as immoral, evil, and bloodthirsty is more important than a nuanced understanding of their behavior and motivations. But that kind of diffusion prevents real insights into complexities and motivations of our enemies beyond just labelling them irrational and evil. Understanding our enemies may be critical to striking political deals with them, but it is difficult to do that when they are evil and we are virtuous; their soldiers are thugs and ours are heroic; their leaders are bloodthirsty and ours are peace loving [13].

Similarly Ward Churchill, a professor at University of Colorado, was fired in 2007 after he published an article arguing that Sep 11 2001 attacks on the US was a response to a long history of US abuses abroad. The decision to fire him did not include a rebuttal of his claims, but instead accused him of plagiarism, and the Colorado legislature called his ideas evil and inflammatory. Of course, evil and inflammatory are value judgements that do not go into the content of the ideas. It appears that some ideas are just too dangerous for wide-spread diffusion, irrespective of their validity. The suppression of some ideas, through economic punishment of their authors, makes it difficult to judge their validity and compare them to the alternative ideas, leaving all intellectually impoverished. Similarly, Laura Kipnis, a professor at Northwestern University, was accused and investigated for sex discrimination, because of her writings criticizing the campus paranoia on sexual harassment and rape culture. Her crime was to write that "on university campuses, the climate of sanctimony about student vulnerability to professors' sexual advances has grown impenetrable. No one dares question it lest you're labeled antifeminist, or worse, a sex criminal." Her job was spared, but presumably her willingness to diffuse dangerous ideas was curtailed significantly, while politically correct ideas are encouraged and widely disseminated. More ominously, the silencing is not always through economic pressure. When foreign countries are involved, silencing can take on a more deadly turn. Anwar Al Awlaki was an American citizen living in Yemen, and the US National Security Agency identified him as a chief propagandists of Al Qaeda in Yemen. He was active on social media advocating violent action against the US and its allies in the Middle East. He was killed in 2011 by a drone strike presumably along with his family. It is not clear if killing people for their political ideas, especially along with their families, constitutes a war crime. But, what is clear is that diffusion of some ideas is very threatening, and challenging them by presenting the opposing ideas is not sufficient to eliminate the threat. Those ideas have to be silenced, and the public need to be protected from them. But that makes it very difficult to understand how our enemies think, and why they are fighting [17, 54].

Wars are not just fought with weapons, but with information. The victory in the Cold War was partly attributed to a lowly radio station called Voice of America that relentlessly broadcasted propaganda to the Soviet population about the good life and prosperity in the capitalist world, never mentioning the misery capitalism was causing in Africa and Latin America. The diffusion was so successful that not even the most ardent critics of capitalism questioned the prosperity brought about by capitalism, despite some extreme suffering in the slums located right next to large capitalist centers. Fighting independence movements in former colonies is also information intensive. First the insurgents are always labelled terrorists, and then they are accused of barbaric acts of violence, and that of course justifies killing them, and sometimes manages to turn their own populations against them. Of course, it is not clear why, when our enemies kill civilians, it is called terrorism, but when we do it with our drone attacks, it is called "collateral damage". When we target political leaders of insurgencies with assassinations, it is called justice, but if they targeted our political leaders for assassination, that would be terrorism. Most activities we call terrorism is indiscriminate killing of civilians, simply because the fighters do not have access to modern precision weapons. When Hamas is accused of shelling Israel indiscriminately, nobody volunteers to give them more precise weapons so that they can target only the military! But when Israel shells Gaza with precision weapons, and still manages to kill many civilians, that is called unavoidable and regrettable collateral damage! The terms we use for ourselves and for our enemies are always different, even when the actions are exactly the same. Our enemies are always terrorists, our friends are freedom fighters even if the tactics are the same. Our enemies are always barbaric when they fight with knives, stones, and improvised crude bombs that kill indiscriminately; but to their supporters they are incredibly brave soldiers fighting against incredible odds with their bare hands, kitchen knives, or with bombs strapped to their own bellies. When ISIS beheads captured soldiers, because they don't want to take prisoners; that is called a barbaric middle ages practice. When we

bombed retreating Iraqi army in the first Iraq war, without giving them the option to surrender, that was called victory! During the Second World War, British and American propaganda machine was boasted as the finest possible. They were successful in portraying the Germans as barbaric, and Hitler as evil. To this day, the Nazi regime is considered the epitome of evil throughout the world, with no attention given to the reasons for the war, why the Nazi regime challenged the dominance of the British Empire, why there was a conflict within Germany between internationalists and the nationalists, and how Jewish population was caught in the middle of that struggle, how moving hostile populations to camps was a standard practice, and how Americans did exactly the same with its Japanese population. The similar issues exist in war torn Syria, where ISIS is constantly accused of killing minorities, when those minorities are precisely the people they are fighting in a war. None of that gets any attention even by some serious historians. Diffusion is very powerful: when you can label your enemies evil and barbaric, half the battle is already won. The following cartoon demonstrates very effectively how terrorist is in the eye of the beholder; one man's terrorist is another man's freedom fighter; and our terrorists are always virtuous and self-sacrificing, but their terrorists are always evil and barbaric [https://www.facebook.com/iamtonystiles/photos/a.1823390751191 85. 43566.153011051385321/1084578821561868/?type=3&theater].

Imagine if Americans had lost the Second World War, and Germans and Japanese were able to write the history. History would read very differently, and would emphasize all the allied atrocities including the carpet bombing of Dresden with tens of thousands of civilian casualties, and the nuclear bombing of Hiroshima and Nagasaki with hundreds of thousands of civilian casualties. The German atrocities to Jews and Gypsies, and Japanese atrocities to Koreans and Chinese would be explained away as necessary collateral damage. After all, winners always write the history. More importantly, if Americans had lost the war, the fate of Japanese Americans would have been very different. The conditions in the internment camps would have deteriorated very quickly, with hunger, disease, and violence, and the fate of Japanese Americans would not have been very different from the German Jews. Once you put people forcefully in internment camps, you have already taken the critical and criminal step towards a lot of misery and suffering. Yet, information wars minimize the importance of that critical first step, and focus on later events which follow naturally from the first step and the outcome of the war. Losers of the war also lose the ability to care for the prisoners in those camps, as supplies are cut off, and resources diminish. No evil intent to exterminate people is necessary to cause untold suffering, although evil intent is often projected to losers by the winners in information wars.

So much information is produced to homogenize the populations of nation states, and to reinforce a national identity. Mandatory education is the primary tool, and it is so effective in diffusing a national identity that most of the time we accept it without even being aware of its artificialness. But in civil wars, when the national identity is challenged, education becomes a salient and powerful tool. Recently, an Afghan girl named Malala became an international hero by advocating education for girls, and suffering attacks by the Afghan Taliban, which was immediately labelled barbaric and medieval for opposing education of girls. Lost in the fervor is the fact that education is not a neutral activity. Education is the primary tool of propaganda and diffusion. All nations use mandatory education to create a national identity by carefully choosing what is taught. Our history is always glorious and full of virtue; our enemies' history is full of vile acts and barbarism. It is no surprise then that Afghan Taliban does not want their girls, or boys for that matter, be educated by the government they are fighting, by an educational system that government controls. Moreover their lifestyle requires girls to be educated differently as homemakers and mothers. To distort cultural differences as evidence of evil, to label resistance to propaganda as oppression of women or minorities are common war tactics. The following cartoon demonstrates the pervasiveness of this tactic in producing untold amount of completely unreliable information [https://www.facebook.com/freetalklive/photos/a.84058224071.87982.65192954071/10152752126789072/?type=1&theater].

Nation-state is an artificial construct. Its major purpose is to wage war more effectively by creating a national myth to rally the population, and to distinguish the population from the enemy. Traditionally, the cultural affinity was centered around family, tribe or city; but with the increasing reach of communication and transportation technologies, it expanded. But a great deal of information is required to maintain such a large and artificial structure, called a national culture. So much of the information generated is not particularly useful or relevant to the population, but it merely creates a common core knowledge to tie them together. As information content grows in scope, it diminishes in specificity, and turns into myths, gods, art, music, movies, celebrities, and athletes. We learn so much about nothing, just to hold the community together, and the information is always tailored to that objective. We know so much about what our soldiers are doing in Afghanistan and their stories of heroism, but know nothing about the Afghan people, how they live, how they die, and their stories of heroism. Actually, we know very little about even our own individual soldiers, their lives, and their suffering. Instead we are bombarded with battles won, future plans, heroic acts committed, numbers killed, but very little about the daily lives of ordinary soldiers. The historian Howard Zinn observing the same tendency to glorify generals and political leaders, while ignoring the ordinary people's lives, wrote an influential book titled "The People's History of the United States", in which he focused on the ordinary people, not the myths created to enforce a national identity by focusing on leaders and celebrities. Information diffusion is a powerful tool in creating identity, and most of the time it is used to create and maintain an artificial national identity [105].

Civil Rights movements also rely on diffusion to establish facts that favor their movements irrespective of reality. Indian independence movement of the early 20th century is often given as a classic example of a non-violent political struggle. Mohandas Karamchand Gandhi is often claimed to be the architect of nonviolent resistance as a successful strategy against a much stronger and more technologically advanced adversary, in this case the British Empire. But it is often ignored that there were many violent resistance movements in early 20th century India, concurrent with the nonviolent movement, some supported by the International adversaries of the British, such as the Russians, and some like Bal Gangadhar Tilak advocating a violent overthrow of the whole British Colonial System. When the British finally accepted defeat, they conveniently credited the nonviolent movement, and discredited the violent resistance. It is often in everybody's interest, when the conflict ends, to reach a negotiated settlement along the lines advocated by the moderates and nonviolent resisters, and to allow them to take credit, for the sake of a final compromise settlement. When in fact, the more extremist and violent movements may have contributed to the struggle equally, if not more, by pressuring the other side to compromise, and push them towards the middle [5].

Similar arguments apply to the Civil Rights Movement of 1960s in the US. The movement glorifies Martin Luther King and his nonviolent movement, but largely ignores the Black Panthers movement during the same period which was organizing riots and sometimes burning large sections of big cities like Los Angeles and Chicago. Their contribution is minimized by historians of the era, although it is doubtful that the nonviolent movement could have succeeded without the violent backdrop, threatening to disrupt the social and economic life of the country, and making the nonviolent approach appear to be the more acceptable, moderate, and compromising solution. Another example is the Irish Independence Movement where the political arm and the military arm of the Irish Republican Army appeared to be at odds in terms of tactics, but in fact, one cannot succeed without the other. Yet another example is the Palestinian Independence struggle against Israel where Palestinian Liberation Organization advocating political settlement and Hamas advocating military resistance appear to be fighting against each other more than the common enemy, but one movement cannot succeed without the other. Every resistance movement needs both a violent military component, and a reconciliatory political movement, to put forward both the threat and the compromise [100].

The rise of the nonviolent approach itself is the result of modern mass communication and coordination technologies that allowed large masses to coordinate boycotts and protests, to inflict enough economic damage to be taken seriously, and to demonstrate and widely diffuse an effective threat of violence, to gain negotiating power.

Information diffusion can also lead to unjustified credibility, and confer advantages to some simply because of the ubiquity and pervasiveness of some information. Just because everybody believes something, does not mean it is true, but in the age of global communication, it is possible to establish some things as facts simply by diffusing them widely, and overloading the receivers to prevent them from critically evaluating the message. Social scientists are frequent perpetrators of such unjustified certainty. In 1980's a large number of clinical psychologists started getting training in the emerging field of child sexual abuse, triggered by a general fear of increased sexualization of children by exposure to increasingly intrusive and sexually explicit public media. Not surprisingly, the more they were trained the more child abuse cases they found, so much so that it quickly became an epidemic. Many children in day care centers, after prodding from clinical psychologists on a moral crusade, started telling bizarre stories of sexual abuse by day care operators. There were claims of bizarre sex acts, often in front of other children, torture in satanic rituals in underground chambers, slaughtering of pets, attacks by robots, molestation by clowns and lobsters, forced eating of pets and frogs, and being tied naked to trees in the school yard. Nobody could verify these stories, yet trained psychologists believed them and testified in courts that these stories were accurate. Many day care operators were convicted of sex crimes and jailed. Meanwhile, the therapists, bolstered by the successes and the consequent increase in demand for their services, and emboldened by their newly found prestige and credibility, sought new ways to discover sexual abuse. They started hypnotizing adult women to help them remember horrifying experiences from their childhood. Women went into therapy with no memory of any trauma, but came out believing that they had been molested by their parents, or tortured in satanic cults, with no corroboration by any siblings, friends, or physicians. With such successes, the therapists received a great deal of media coverage. The more information came out in the media, the more sex abuse cases were filed, and the more people believed them. Quantity overwhelmed the quality of information, and increased media coverage of successes eliminated all skepticism, and led to unjustified certainty and overconfidence. All of these claims were later found to be false, and after years of wrangling and debate, the jailed were exonerated and eventually freed [80].

The whole field of psychoanalysis also benefitted greatly from diffusion. Starting with its inventor, Sigmund Freud, it found a huge following among the professional therapists, not because it was particularly effective, but it was the fashionable approach promoted by a big name. It has largely been abandoned now in favor of behavior modification and drug therapies. Looking back, it is hard to understand how it could have been so popular with such a dismal record, except for the diffusion effect. It was too expensive, too slow, and demanded too much intellectual sophistication from the patient, to be considered an effective therapy. It is very disconcerting to hear from one of the famous practitioners of the approach, Leon Wurmser, that one of his patients abruptly broke off analysis in the 1172nd session, another remained in analysis faithfully for eleven years, and a third one killed himself by jumping off of a bridge. Psychoanalysis became interminable, and often ended in failure, sometimes after years of intensive therapy. Yet the practice survived a long time, as long as there were many practitioners who believed in it and made a living at it, which encouraged many others to believe in it and make a living at it [113].

Information diffuses fast when it justifies our political interests or confirms our existing beliefs, not necessarily when it discovers the truth. Child molestation hysteria involved both the political interests and preexisting beliefs of therapists, and diffused like wild fire. Colonialism as a political tool had the same characteristics. It was justified as civilizing the indigenous people, and confirmed both the existing beliefs about the backwardness of indigenous people; and also served the political interests of colonial powers in subjugating the indigenous people. It perpetuated a system of exploitation by transferring some technologies to enable to local population to participate in the global economy, yet making sure that they were never fully capable of competing with the global powers. It created elites in those countries that participated in the global economy, and aided in the exploitation of their own masses. Weapons transfers also followed the same model, with sufficient transfers to allow the locals to fight the Western wars and pay for the weapons with their resources, but never enough to challenge the Western powers directly. To this day, nuclear, biological, and long range missile technologies are always kept away from the upcoming nations to keep them militarily inferior. As colonialism became increasingly difficult to sustain because of the diffusion of deadly weapons, and the communication technologies making it easier for the masses to organize, it was replaced by modern multinational corporate capitalism that created an elite capitalist class in third world countries that represented the local interests of global corporations, and in exchange were supported economically and even militarily in the exploitation of their own masses. This is how corporate and military power of western empires often collaborated with third word dictatorships, but the moral arguments about civilization and democracy dominated all arguments about economic and military interventions, greatly confusing their own populations about the real purposes of such interventions. The following cartoon captures the subtlety of language in referring to colonialism, terrorism, religion, and other politically charged terms [https://www.facebook.com/inedibleindia1/photos/a.86770053995046 4.1073741827.867695293284322/914256711961513/?type=3&theate r].

Colonialism was justified in terms of the superiority of the Europeans over indigenous people. The evidence for superiority was extensive and indisputable, if you define superiority as technological development to manipulate and exploit nature. Such self-serving definitions are very common, and the resulting body of knowledge all support the starting hypothesis, because initial hypotheses are always self-serving, and subsequently the information sought is always the confirming evidence for the starting hypothesis. Alternative hypotheses are almost never considered, and the disconfirming evidence is almost never sought, because hypothesis generation is not a science, and the evidence collection is always guided by the initial hypothesis. No European would test the hypothesis that indigenous people had superior social structures that reduced or even eliminated crime, loneliness, and mental illness, since that would be counter-intuitive and self-defeating. Modern science is no different in its effort to generate hypotheses and seek evidence, neither of which is scientific, but only the analysis of the gathered evidence is. This social context of scientific discovery has been studied in great detail and found to be largely non-scientific and biased [47]. No scientist is going to seriously investigate such counter-intuitive and politically threatening subjects such as whether polygamy leads to better outcomes for children, or if recreational drugs and sex may be beneficial to teen development, or if agricultural slavery may have been better for the American slaves than the industrial wage-work that replaced it, or if Germany may have been justified in challenging the monopoly of the British Empire on the natural resources of the world by starting the Second World war, or ISIS may be fighting a justified war of self-defense for the Sunni populations of Iraq and Syria.

Academic debates are also similarly dependent on definitions and initial assumptions. The philosophical debate of existence versus essence posited by existentialism is a classic example of an unending debate which is critically dependent on definitions and assumptions. The answer to this enduring dilemma is simply either we don't know, or it is both, depending on how you define existence and essence, but no philosopher will subscribe to those easy answers because their livelihood and prestige depends on the complexity of the answer and the ambiguity of initial definitions. Moreover, science may have answered this question, but philosophers are not likely to be satisfied with simple answers. The debate goes back to theological arguments about humans having an essence, or a soul, that gives meaning to their existence. That debate has been settled by modern biological sciences which discredited soul and grand purpose arguments. The more modern version of this dilemma is merely a nature versus nurture debate, as to whether humans have an essence that naturally defines the meaning of their life, or they merely exist without any grand purpose, but cerate purpose themselves. The answer is clearly both, as there is ample scientific evidence that humans have evolved to exhibit some behaviors, and yet they are flexible enough to learn and adapt other behaviors. The grand purpose of life in some sense is living the life we have evolved to live, yet the flexibility of that design gives us some room to maneuver and define our own life purposes, like serving your country. Yet, such a simple resolution will not be considered by philosophers, as their academic traditions diffuse complexity as a self-serving tool, and their initial definitions leftover from an earlier era of theological philosophy reinforces itself by eliciting only confirming evidence for the initial hypotheses.

One can make similar arguments for many fundamental debates dominating humanities, and the liberal arts education. We are often told that a liberal arts education makes us more humane, more tolerant, and even more human. Living aside the problems with what that means, and whether it is desirable, one needs more specific arguments why studying Homer, or Shakespeare, or Sartre makes us more human! In a fast changing technological world, the world these historical figures faced is long gone. Their theories depended on definitions and assumptions of their time. If the world has changed, and if we don't fight with swords, challenge each other to duels, or worry about our souls anymore, are they still relevant, or more precisely, do what degree they are relevant? That has to be clearly articulated before one can accept the argument that humanities are important to human education. It is not enough that they have diffused our literature; it is not enough to argue that everybody should study them simply because everybody studies them! But that is what diffusion does by establishing facts just because they are commonly believed for some historical reason! Just look at the following picture titled Achilles Slays Hector by Peter Paul Rubens circa 1630, demonstrating a subject studied intensely by all students of classics, and forms a basic building block of any liberal arts education [https://www.facebook.com/GreekPhilosophers/photos/a.5646853868 98506.1073741829.468386006528445/564688076898237/?type=3&t heater].

Is that the world we face today? How much of their thoughts and ideas are relevant today? Are there really any basic human conditions and truths that are universal, so we can learn from this education? Or is it all arbitrary conditions diffusing universally, simply because they already diffused far and wide, and achieved a critical mass, just by being at the right place at the right time in history [3]?

The philosophical debates over the meaning of life, and the meaninglessness of the modern life has been raging on for several centuries now. Numerous philosophers from Nietzsche to Sartre, and social scientists from Freud to Weber have lamented the fact that modern life had alienated humans from grand purposes such as religion and god, leading to a loss of meaning. Science and humanism were not able to replace the lost meaning by providing an overarching explanation for life and its purpose, leading to a morality vacuum and numerous psychological disorders. The debates centered on whether religion was critical to humans, and if not, what it could be replaced with. The answer was not forthcoming after several hundred years of debate. In fact, the answer is quite simple once the diagnosis is done correctly. As important as religion is in organizing large numbers of people into collective action, and it may have been the single most important factor in the success of human species because it enabled large scale cooperation, religion is not critical to a purpose in life. Its explanations about god's intent for human life are secondary to building a community with shared beliefs. After all, animals live quite purposeful and productive lives without a grand meaning and religious experience. The loss of meaning and purpose in modern life is due to the breakdown of extended family and community. Community is what gives meaning to human life, because humans are social animals like all other great apes. Industrial revolution led to a loss of purpose and meaning because of the mobility and specialization it required, and the subsequent breakdown of geographically based family and community ties. The coincidental breakdown of religion is merely a coincidence, simply because the industrial revolution was fueled by the scientific revolution which happen to also challenge the religious doctrine. The solution to the moral malaise, and psychological deadening of the soul then is simply to reestablish a sense of community and belonging. Religion, tribes, extended families are only some of the methods used in the past. Nationalism, professional sports, and music are some of the newer methods to build communities. But possibilities are endless in building living and learning communities with shared space, communal food and shelter, shared activities of business, farming, or professions, shared child rearing and many others. The objective is to build permanent, stable, yet flexible communities to create a sense of belonging without avoiding the requirements of a modern mobile and specialized lifestyle. Such effective social change requires correct identification of the problem, and new creative lifestyle solutions, not a debate among old ideologies.

Philosophers often take credit for social change, simply because they debate them to no end. In fact social change takes place because new technologies and new organizational arrangements make them economically or politically favorable to powerful groups, not because of philosophical arguments. The decline of religion is one such social change, caused primarily by a powerful challenge to the church by nation-states; yet that did not stop various philosophers from taking credit for the decline of religion. The following cartoon demonstrates that humorously [https://www.facebook.com/8bitphilosophy/photos/a.323798501113502 .1073741828.288221834671169/533690456790971/?type=3&theater].

Free Will is another such concept that is fiercely debated, yet poorly understood. It was also left over from the theological debates of another era of whether humans were free agents capable of making decisions, or if they were merely instruments of god, to exercise its will, who set a destiny and fate for them. Modern versions of this debate involve whether humans can control their environment, or if they are merely observers of nature as it follows its own trajectory. The answer once again depends on how you define free will, as it is a poorly defined concept like most such philosophical concepts. If it is merely a capability to make decisions, all humans have that capability, and even robots and computer programs do also. All humans do some things automatically with no control, like heartbeat, digestive processes, dreams, and feelings of pain when injured; and clearly they make choices about other things like what to wear, what career to follow, who to marry, and what to eat. But, that capability to make decisions itself is learned and captured as decision processes, using already existing learning capabilities, so the decisions themselves would be completely predictable if one has access to sufficient information about someone's background in terms of what they have inherited genetically and what they have been exposed to throughout their lives. Decisions we make clearly follow some internal procedures that take our observations as input and produce decisions. Those procedures are learned and predictable, if there is sufficient information. The only way they may not be predictable is if there is some randomness. If free will is defined as acting independently of our environment, then the only known way for that to happen is by randomness. But randomness does not confer the power of free will to the individual, because randomness itself is a built-in procedure. If there is a way to act independently of our environment, but not randomly, we don't know how that would be possible, and no amount of debate will figure it out! The answer is simply not known. Yet, diffusion of such debates have their own inertia that keeps them alive, because it keeps debaters in business, and gives them academic careers and intellectual leadership positions.

If free will is merely an illusion, where does it come from and why is it so pervasive? Imagine a robot that moves right or left after observing a right or left turn signal. That is immediately perceived as a simple procedure and no free will is imputed to the robot. Now imagine that the robot observes not only the external turn signal, but also some internal state like its remaining battery power, and turns only if it has enough battery power left. Now, an outside observer may impute some free will to the robot, because that internal state is not visible to him, and it appears that robot is behaving somewhat independent of its observations. Now imagine a more complex procedure where the robot observes both the external and internal signals, and if it has enough battery power, it follows the turn signal 90% of the time, but does not turn 10% of the time. This introduction of randomness would clearly cause the outside observer to conclude that the robot was behaving relatively independent of its observations by introducing its own will. In fact it is an illusion. Free will is an illusion caused by hidden observations and randomness.

Simone De Beauvoir, the famous existentialist philosopher, once said that women are not born, they are made. She is probably wrong. Many feminist activists applauded this statement, and argued that gender is not fixed, but constructed. Once again, the answer is straightforward, and does not require unending debate and extensive diffusion of arguments to serve political ideals. To suggest that individuals can use their free will to define gender is probably wrong, since free will itself is an illusion! Gender has three components: Inherited part, socially constructed part, and individually defined part. To focus on one or the other to the exclusion of others is misleading. Yes, you are born a woman with the physical and chemical structures that make someone a woman. There may be a spectrum, and there may be some with ambiguous gender identity, but that does not change the overarching biological factors. Women give birth, men don't! No philosophical debate is going to change that. On top of that, social constructs define gender roles. Why a woman does housework and a man goes to war is a social construct. It could be changed to some extent, although with great difficulty since there are often historical or economic reasons why! Individual choice is only the third component where a woman may choose one role or another as long as it is socially accepted and biologically possible. This is very limited freedom, and given that free will itself is an illusion, most women can only exercise that freedom to the extent that they have learned about that possibility, and their social context allows it, and learning and social context is not under their control. No Saudi woman is going to walk around naked; or no American man could either for that matter, without being severely sanctioned and socially rejected. That is not a choice available, or even recognized as possible, philosophical debates aside. What choices are available are often determined by historical events and technological trajectories that follow their own logic. It is easy to see for example that the options available to women have enlarged because of a variety of technologies that automated housework and allowed birth control. Those technologies followed their own trajectories and internal logic, relatively independent of any individual woman's desire for a different gender role.

Law enforcement also suffers from frequent overconfidence when faced with a flood of self-justifying and self-selected information. The self-selected evidence can be so convincing that it can be even used to convince the suspects of their own guilt even when they are completely innocent. People often wonder why anyone would possibly confess to a crime that they did not commit. In fact it is quite common, especially when police presents overwhelming evidence about their guilt, often completely and deliberately false evidence, which overwhelms the suspect's own perception of the facts. Interrogators are routinely encouraged to present false evidence to a suspect, adopt the attitude of "Don't lie, we know you are guilty", and reject the suspect's denials. Reid Technique of police interrogations encourages police officers to tell the suspect that their finger prints were on the weapon, the victim's blood was on their shirt, or an eye witness saw them at the crime scene. Then the interrogators are encouraged to provide explanations to the confusion they created in the suspect's mind, like possibly he committed the crime and blanked it out, or maybe he has multiple personalities. Information is a powerful tool and those who control your information can control your mind even when the information contradicts your own personal experience [80].

According to one study, out of 125 cases where prisoners were later exonerated, 80% of them were interrogated in this fashion for more than 6 hours, and half more than 12 hours non-stop. Central Park Jogger Case was one of these cases where five teenagers confessed to a brutal rape and assault of a young woman in 1989 after long hours of leading and misleading questioning by the police. After being convicted and serving several years in jail, all were found to be innocent. But such reversals come years after the convictions. Until then, in the short run, these are success stories for the law enforcement. As such success stories diffuse through the law enforcement community, they become the modus operandi, since nobody can afford to ignore a technique that works so well, and risk being labelled incompetent, even if it leads to false convictions, and be reversed eventually. In a competitive environment, short run success always dominates people's decisions; long run consequences are always far away in the distance [80].

CHAPTER 11

OVERLOAD

Some things are better not known.

More information is not always better. In a competitive environment, too much information overwhelms the decision makers, and leads to random elimination of options, to reduce the load to manageable portions, and make decisions in a timely fashion. In a famous experiment, marketing researchers presented an array of jams to a panel of consumers to taste, and to choose from for purchase. One group was presented with three types of jams, and the other was presented with seven. Those who were presented with three types made a decision and bought one twice as frequently. The explanation is that more choice is not necessarily better. When you have more choices, you may find it much more difficult to make a decision, and avoid the decision. If you are forced to make a decision, you may arbitrarily eliminate some relevant attributes from consideration.

Career decisions are often very complex with an innumerable number of criteria to consider. Facing such impossible information processing tasks, most people narrow their choices randomly to specific geographic areas, specific fields that pay well, or simply the fields they have been exposed to and liked. Career counselors, facing the same insurmountable task, often recommend young people to follow their heart, and go into a field they love. But to love something as complex as a field of study requires extensive exposure to it. To limit your criteria to the things you have already been exposed to and loved at first sight is very shortsighted. Careers are often too complex for love at first sight; you learn to love them over decades.

Shortcuts are also very common when people are overloaded with political messages. Labels and images are substituted for the content, and used as shortcuts for decision making instead of the real information. In one experiment, Israelis and Palestinians were given the other side's proposals in a negotiation session. When it was labelled as their own government's proposal they overwhelmingly approved it. When the proposal was labelled correctly as the other side's proposal, they overwhelmingly rejected it. It is very common in political debates, the supporters of one candidate find every proposal by others unacceptable, and even stupid; yet when the same idea is proposed by their own candidate, it is overwhelmingly approved, or even considered brilliant. President Obama's healthcare plan, when it was adopted by a republican governor, Mitt Romney, the republicans of the state considered it a brilliant move by a moderate republican. When the same proposal was made by President Obama, Massachusetts republicans almost unanimously opposed it as a government takeover of health care. Labels are often a poor substitute for understanding and analyzing the content, but information overload makes them necessary [80]. Humor is often used as a political weapon by labelling opponents with memorable shortcuts, instead of long and complex arguments. The following cartoon demonstrates how political humor can be very effective in subjecting a political candidate to ridicule by labelling and shortcuts, instead of making substantive arguments. This cartoon is about the republican candidate Donald Trump in the 2016 presidential election, combining his fascistic tendencies and his unusual hairdo in one memorable label [https://www.instagram.com/p/_FIdXWELcV/].

The same arguments apply to spouse selection. Faced with an impossible task of finding a lover among many friends, acquaintances, friends of friends, professional contacts, online liaisons, and many potential mates in dating sites, one cannot possibly make an informed decision. Almost everybody develops shortcuts and rules of thumb as to their preferences. Most of these shortcuts relate to appearance because it is easily visible; others relate to their education or job because they can be easily ascertained; some go as far as considering their hobbies, clothes they wear, and cars they drive; but anything beyond that, especially involving complex character traits, communication style, and lifestyle choices are simply ignored, to be considered later. Early elimination has to be on the basis of superficial traits that can be judged easily; but then they tend to dominate the decisions because if you can't survive the early elimination, the later and more sophisticated criteria are irrelevant. This is the reason why most everybody lies in their online dating profiles, because surviving the initial superficial screening is critical to getting a date, even if you have to explain and backtrack later.

These shortcuts in spouse selection distort the decisions dramatically, so much so that the quality of decisions may be worse than those involving prearranged marriages in traditional societies.

After all, the divorce rates in arranged; marriages are much lower than marriages self-selection. Why would individual freedom and consent lead to a worse decisions than a decision imposed on you? It sounds like a contradiction in terms. In fact, consent may not always be desirable, especially when decisions are complex and information overload is a real possibility, and others can make the decision more rationally and more effectively than you can for yourself. Consent assumes that you have complete information and you can process it rationally. Neither of those is true in general. We don't require consent to education by children. If we did very few children would get education. We don't consent to being born; we don't consent to wearing clothes and covering our genitals; we don't consent to our citizenship. Do we consent to military service, or is it imposed on us through economic pressure or even conscription? Do we consent to marriage or is it imposed on us through social norms? Do we consent to our religion or is it imposed on us by our parents? Do we consent to paying taxes? Do we consent to wearing a suit to work? Most of our behavior does not involve explicit consent but it is imposed on us by

laws, social rules, and economic pressure. And how would you consent to something you have never done before? How would a young person consent to sex if she has never done it before, except by caving in to pressure by peers and lovers? It is possible to provide education to facilitate these decisions, but then education has to be unbiased and also concise enough to avoid overload. It almost never is! There is a tremendous incentive to control education to bias others' information to serve your interests. In fact, controlling others' information is as effective as using force in controlling behavior. Consent creates an illusion of freedom, but often with no real freedom.

Consider consent to sex that has become a rallying cry of feminists in overcoming what they consider to be a rape culture where men try to bypass explicit consent as much as possible. Explicit consent before any sex sounds wonderful, but it becomes unworkable very quickly, unless there is considerable sexual freedom, and sex is rather routine, and consent is easy to obtain. But if sex is a complex transaction with many implicit obligations, consent is not easy. Compare it to commercial transactions where consent is also necessary. If it is the purchase of an apple in the farmer's market, consent and agreement is easy to establish. Some coins will be exchanged, and if credit has to be extended for a few minutes for one party to go get change, a hand shake will suffice. But then consider a real estate transaction with many concerns and obligations extending over a period of time. Then lawyers and bankers are involved, documents are signed, and obligations are clearly defined. Is sex more like the first or the second? Sexual mores are changing, and sex is increasingly being liberated from the strict controls that existed before birth control technologies. But it is far from a routine simple exchange, free from future expectations and obligations. And to the extent that it is not free and routine, it will not lend itself to simple consent without formal written contracts.

Traditional societies rely on explicit rules of conduct that regulate sexual activity, typically involving a formal agreement like marriage, or an informal understanding laid out in traditions, that lay out all the social, sexual, emotional, and financial obligations. That simplifies the decisions by restricting the freedom of the individuals. Replacing such strict rules with consent requires complex negotiations before each sexual activity, and leads to information overload very quickly. Not only it is very inefficient, but the difficulty of establishing meaningful consent leads to misunderstandings, unjustified expectations, and cynicism. It damages people psychologically, and makes them bitter and angry. Ironically, the freedom from strict gender roles and easing of sexual restrictions limit your freedom, by making you a slave of information overload through constant negotiation of sexual expectations and constantly reinventing the wheel of social rules. Traditions and restrictions limit your options but also free you from constant information processing, decision making, and negotiation. Consent based sexual freedom can only work when sex is a routine and simple activity without future expectations and obligations.

Scientific research also suffers from information overload, as it is increasingly difficult to glean reliable scientific conclusions from an avalanche of articles that claim many variations of the same fact under a variety of different conditions and assumptions, or even outright contradict each other. As the scientific literature proliferates, it is increasingly difficult to figure out what is scientifically established, what is likely to be true, what is tentatively suggested, what is an educated guess, and what is pure speculation. Reputable scientists engage in all of these with no serious attempt to label them correctly. For decades, cholesterol in diet was condemned as the primary cause of cardiovascular disease. New evidence shows that those scientific claims may have been completely unjustified. More ominously, the substitutes that were created for cholesterol, such as trans-fats, may have actually caused more harm to human health. For decades, scientists encouraged the population to have a low-fat and high-carb diet for weight loss and other health benefits. New evidence suggests that a high-fat and low-carb diet may be better for weight loss. For many decades, medical researchers recommended aggressive treatment of prostate and breast cancers with aggressive surgical removal of affected and surrounding tissue. New evidence suggests that for many such cancers a "wait and see" approach may work better, since they might be non-aggressive and slow-spreading cancers. Climate scientists have been arguing for several decades now what the eventual impact of climate change might be. Some are convinced that a catastrophic flooding of most land base is the most likely outcome; others are sure that it will be as little as one-foot rise in sea levels [43].

There are similar debates on nutritional value and safety of the various foods. There are vegan diets, gluten free diets, soy free diets, debates over the dangers of antibiotics in the food, fat content, saturated fat content, trans fat content, arguments over eating only raw food, avoiding genetically modified foods, emphasizing low carb or low fat foods, and a whole variety of other issues. All of these became issues during the past fifty years. Before then, every community had traditional diets and methods of producing food, and everybody in the community followed those traditions and standards that were established and tried over millennia. Is it possible to make reasonable decisions about one's diet in such an information overload environment especially when much of the information is confusing, misleading, or downright wrong? The following cartoon demonstrates the issue nicely with the caption of "Finally settling down to my vegan, gluten free, soy free, antibiotics free, raw, non GMO, organic, fat free, low carb meal!" [https://www.facebook.com/photo.php?fbid=738397766288079&set= gm.1096150917063127&type=1&theater].

Science is lauded with its ability to be self-correcting, as all conclusions are tentative, and new findings can confirm or deny the old conclusions, constantly modifying our beliefs according to new evidence. But such a process is useful only if error rates are low, and corrections arrive relatively fast. In a world where most research findings are false, and corrections do not arrive for decades, science would quickly lose its credibility. If erroneous scientific findings can last for decades without a serious challenge, then it is a small consolation that science is eventually self-correcting. Modifying an old legal maxim, we could say: Correction delayed is correction denied! It is much more important to get it right the first time, but science is increasingly producing an overload of tentative results. In an overload environment, with constant pressure to discover new and surprising facts, we are bombarded with new research findings that are mere unexplained correlations, or even accidental data anomalies. Every research paper now ends with an exhortation to do more research to validate the findings. The conclusive validations are hard to come by, forever delayed, or completely nonexistent [102].

Academic world has become an information factory where thousands of low wage laborers toil under difficult conditions with very little reliable output to show for it. American Psychological Association published the following joke to demonstrate the problem of too much output, too little accomplishment. A recently deceased psychologist arrived at the pearly gates, where St. Peter greeted him and promptly offered him the choice of heaven or hell. Taken aback, all the psychologist could manage to say was, "Well, may I at least have a look at each before deciding?" "Of course," said St. Peter, and so guided the psychologist down a long escalator. At the bottom of the ride, the psychologist saw row upon row of desks in an airplane hangar–sized room, each attended by a hunched academic, furiously typing on a laptop. "Yes, that's pretty grim," agreed the psychologist. "I can't imagine spending an eternity like that; let me see heaven." Riding up the long escalator, his excitement began to build. However, his mouth fell open when at the top of it he again stared out at a vast hall of identical academics, all pounding away on keyboards. "I don't understand," was all he could manage to say. "But don't you see?" said St. Peter, "It is completely different. These scholars are getting their papers published" [26].

Modern wars are also information intensive, and that emphasis on information often detracts from the real objectives, with dire consequences. Incredible amounts of data were collected during Vietnam War. We always killed more of the enemy than the enemy killed of us; we won every battle; yet we lost the war! Military made a point of keeping track of every detail, and ensuring the military assets were deployed efficiently, and specific targets were always reached. In the process, they lost sight of why we were fighting and what losses were worth taking for us; as opposed to why the enemy was fighting and what losses were worth taking for them. We were fighting for colonial dominance half a world away; they were fighting for national survival in their backyard. That distinction was lost in the minute details of the battlefield tactics. More information often substitutes detail for substance, tactics for strategies, and means for ends. More information is dangerous, because it can blind you to substance. It can force you to compete on the basis of immediate information for short term advantages, but a collection of short term advantages do not always add up to long term advantages. As a result, you can win all the battles, yet lose the war!

In justifying wars, the leaders also resort to symbolic arguments with an overload of imagery, rather than concise and precise arguments, because overload is very effective in blocking critical judgement. Ronald Reagan was called the great communicator precisely because of his ability to use sensory rich imagery and examples, instead of parsimonious arguments. His justification for the Vietnam War was a classic example of this, when he gave a speech overlooking the Arlington National Cemetery, and pointed out that honorable men had given their lives for the cause, and gave many specific examples of heroism. That was his justification for the war. He made no arguments for the wisdom of that war and what was accomplished strategically, yet was very effective in convincing the masses that it was a just war. This is a very common tactic with great leaders. Imagery and symbolism may not be good substitutes for arguments in an intellectual debate; but they are very effective and quite convincing at public debates because they operate at a subconscious level. Precise arguments invite counter-arguments; images and vivid examples overload our senses and suppress our counter-arguments [80].

One such symbolic argument is victimhood. Victimhood became a powerful argument for collective action, when only a few hundred years ago, claiming victimhood would only get you ridicule and abuse. Historically, people were expected to stand up and fight, and if they lose, accept their fate and surrender. Victims are the new heroes who endure abuse and seek justice without violence, but by eliciting sympathy. It only works in an information rich environment, where we need shortcuts to identify political struggles, and solve them before they become violent and lead to lose-lose outcomes. Victimhood is a protest, claiming injustice, and possibly threatening violence without resorting to it. In that respect, it is similar to protest movements where the aggrieved parties announce their grievances publicly as in demonstrations and marches, without taking violent action. The victims demand justice and sacrifice from others, with an implicit threat of violence. In an information overload environment, victimhood is a very effective shortcut to elicit support. The state of Israel is a result of a sustained campaign by European Jews proclaiming victimhood as a result of Second World War, and eliciting an international response to their plight, including major financial support from Germany. The modern Palestinian statehood movement also heavily relies on a theory of victimhood as a result of being driven from their lands by the Israeli government. Ironically, the new Palestinian movement emulates the victimhood movement that worked successfully for the state of Israel, and uses it against Israel. The fact that they moved away from the exclusively violent resistance to occupation and adopted victimhood as a better strategy is a testament to the power of that strategy in the modern world. The modern feminist movement is also largely based on the theory of female victimhood in the hands of males in a patriarchal and male-dominated society that denied them their basic rights. It is not clear if division of labor, and strict roles on the basis of gender, are necessarily oppressive without understanding the economic details of those arrangements; nevertheless the female victimhood is overwhelmingly accepted as the reality of our human past and even in our current social organization. It is often ignored that homemaking used to be a difficult and prestigious job that also paid well through the economic partnership of marriage, before the advent of household automation with electricity, electric appliances and indoor plumbing. Homemaking as oppression may be a modern phenomenon resulting from large scale automation of housework, leading to a loss of prestige in housework, and also diminished interest in reproduction and large families. Victimhood can be a very powerful strategy to organize not just the victims, but also to pressure the alleged victimizers to atone and make reparations, with merely imagery and symbolism, instead of detailed and precise arguments.

Advertising industry uses the same tactics to block resistance and counterarguments. Any advertisement that argues that Coca Cola gives you energy and improves your mood is likely to be resisted with counterarguments. But an advertisement that shows lots of young and beautiful people playing volleyball on the beach with great vigor while drinking Coca Cola engenders no such counter-argument, because it registers its message at a subconscious level. Similarly, any advertisement that argues that cigarette smoking makes you tough and independent would be resisted; but a masculine looking cowboy smoking a cigarette registers the association between the two very effectively. Imagery and vivid examples overload our senses, and drill their messages directly into our subconscious with no critical evaluation on or part [80].

There is considerable evidence that symbolic or implied conclusions, as opposed to explicit arguments, are much more effective in convincing the audience, and also more difficult to reverse. Two psychologists at Kent State University conducted an experiment where they gave two versions of a crime story to students. One claimed that there was a burglary in the home of an elderly couple, and their son was implicated. The other also reported the burglary, but only said that they had a son who had gambling debts, only implying that he might have been involved. Later, the subjects were told that the son had an alibi. At the end of the experiment, the subjects were asked who might have committed the crime. Those who were given the story explicitly implicating the son were much more likely to accept the alibi and exonerate the son; and those who were given a vague implication that the son might have been involved were much more likely to suspect the son. Implied and symbolic information is much more convincing because it breaks our resistance to propaganda, by creating the illusion that we have reached our own conclusions; because it allows us to fill in the blanks for ourselves, even if those blank fillers are preordained and inescapable by the symbolic information provided [45].

Sometimes, a highly salient piece of information forces a specific decision that is not necessarily optimum; but lack of it, or ignorance, allows better decision making. Three days after the 2010 earthquake in Haiti, a Royal Caribbean cruise ship docked in Haiti, sixty miles from the earthquake zone. Passengers enjoyed water sports, a barbeque, and shopped for Haitian handcrafts. But when the news of the earthquake arrived at the ship, and the passengers found out that down the coast a few dozen miles, tens of thousands of Haitians were being buried in mass graves, some passengers refused disembark and join the festivities. They could not see themselves frolicking on the beach, when there was such a catastrophe down the coast. Yet, before the news arrived, they were quite happy with the festivities; and refusing to join in the festivities did no one any good. It was not the optimum decision, but the additional information made it a moral imperative for many passengers. Some passengers wanted to divert the ship away from the disaster zone, and dock at Bahamas, so that they could enjoy themselves without the guilt of playing so close to the disaster zone. But again, doing so would not do any good for anyone. Additional information was forcing a non-optimum decision, for fear of being criticized as callous and non-caring [62].

Information often promotes unnecessary competition, and lack of it encourages cooperation. More importantly, as more information encourages competition, competition encourages production of even more information, leading to information wars. The 17th century French missionary Paul Le Jeune was shocked about the sexual promiscuity of Native Americans and how they would often engage in group sex during their dances and festivals. He chastised a chief for permitting this and said not only it was a sin, but it was stupid, because he probably did not even know if his children were really his! The chief responded: "You Europeans are so stingy with your love. You love only your own children. We love all the children of our tribe as if they are our own. So, it doesn't matter if they are really mine!" [85]. Similarly, biologist Richard Dawkins asks: "Why do we limit ourselves to one romantic partner? We love multiple children, and tell them there is no need to be jealous as there is enough parental love for all of them. We are never exclusive in our love of books, food, wine, vacations, and music. Why is romantic love an exception?" The information about the ownership of children often leads to competition for sex and destructive jealousy. The lack of that information leads to cooperation and love for all, leading to a more harmonious society, with more access to sex for all, and more care for children. More importantly, once you know the parentage of children, there is an incentive to create even more information to gain some competitive advantage over others' children, ranging from intelligence tests to competitive sports to artistic competitions, leading to a vicious cycle of constant ranking of children in terms of their ability and accomplishments. Some things are better not known [85]!

Monogamy may have originated from a desire to curtail competition among men for women. Competition for women can be vicious throughout the animal world, and humans are no exception, as sex is a primary need for humans, and maximizing reproduction is a major survival trait. Traditional warfare was often caused for access to sex; and the women of the losing side were almost always taken for sex and reproduction. As late as Middle Ages, it was common for men to duel each other to death over access to women. Even in modern times, it is not unusual for men to commit violence to gain and maintain access to women, whether it is rape, or bar fights over women. Monogamy curbs that violence by restricting each men to only one woman. The restriction goes far beyond marriage, but limits how much you can know about possible partners. Limited knowledge limits competition. In the traditional prearranged marriages, a man really knows only one woman as there is no interaction between men and women, so competition among men is severely curtailed by a lack of information. In modern relationships, there is more information available through dating and friendships, but there is a constant effort to limit the amount of information available to limit competition. Clothing and body covering is primarily an effort to limit information available about your body. Women go to great lengths to make sure not all of their body is available for viewing, and limit that access to those who have made certain commitments. That has the effect of limiting competition among men to whatever information is made available, and women are careful to manipulate that information with make-up and choice of clothing so that they reveal only the favorable information. Also limiting the times when a women's body is available for viewing limits the sexual competition to those times. Women reveal more when they are courting men to encourage more competition, and reveal less when they are not, to control and manipulate the competition. Traditional Moslem women reveal very little of their body to the general public. That limits the competition among men severely, and forces them to make marriage decisions without considering appearance and beauty, but solely on the basis of family connections. It is important to limit information and sexual competition in an environment where resources are scarce and cooperation is critical to survival. Traditional African women on the other hand, reveal most of their body freely to the public. That encourages sexual competition. That is useful in a resource rich environment where competition is affordable. Most societies fall somewhere in the middle, and limit body exposure to varying degrees at different times and places. Genitals are almost always covered, to limit sexual activity and sexual competition to specific times and locations, and also to redirect the competition. Exposure of genitals and body parts would unduly emphasize genitalia and body shape in sexual competition, at the expense of other criteria such as economic and social status. Those with economic and social status have all the incentive to force everyone to cover their genitals through social norms they create, to change the nature of competition in their favor. Similarly, dress codes and uniforms are widely used to limit information about our bodies and limit competition to specific tasks. Military and police uniforms, business suits, and hospital garb all signal specific tasks at hand, and limit all other involvement. Covering our bodies with specific clothing is an effort to limit information about our bodies and to dedicate our bodies to specific tasks. Otherwise unlimited information would lead to constant competition for our attention and for our bodies by many tasks and many participants.

Dating and mating practices have always operated under limited information. It is impossible to know very much about a potential mate, before spending a lot of time with him, and it is difficult to do that with many potential mates. Modern electronic communication is changing it. Dating services contain huge amounts of information about millions of people. But that creates an overload as it is impossible to carefully evaluate and compare that many alternatives. The solution is often to focus on one superficial feature to quickly eliminate many alternatives. That superficial feature is always the appearance. Tinder, following many others like Hinge, OK Cupid, and Lulu, is the latest dating application for phones that takes this approach by presenting just the pictures of potential dates with minimal information, and the customers merely swipe yes or no until they find a match. But focusing on a single feature, creates a winner-take-all market, because you can easily sort the thousands of options on that one criteria, and everybody wants the top ranking option. There is evidence that Tinder creates a few very successful daters with hundreds of dates a month, and the rest get practically nothing [86]. The same problem exists in recommendation systems based on rankings. Trip Advisor and Yelp provide overall aggregate rankings for restaurants and hotels, but that only creates winner-take-all markets as everybody wants to go to the top ranking restaurant or hotel, irrespective of the differences among them, and the desirability and relevance of different features to different individuals. US News and World Report publishes aggregate rankings for colleges, and that similarly creates a winner-take-all market for the best students. This is why more information is not necessarily better, because it artificially focuses decision making on a few arbitrary and superficial characteristics to reduce overload. This is why mate selection in traditional societies is made by match makers who have the time and the expertise to look at multiple factors, and the individuals have limited access to information about potential mates until the wedding day. Body covering, gender separation, social restrictions on mixed gender activities are all designed to limit information about potential mates to prevent information overload, superficial decision making, and winner-take-all markets. In modern mating, females exposing their bodies to potential mates on a beach, leads to a few women with model bodies dominating the mate selection process. Ironically, feminists who advocate women's freedom to expose their bodies as they like, and criticize harshly the conservative societies like Saudi Arabia, Iran, and Afghanistan that limit women's ability to expose their bodies, also complain about the obsession with body image, and women being judged solely by their body shape in mate selection. But the very freedom they advocate encourages, and even forces women to compete on the basis of body shape, as information overload limits men's ability to make a more careful evaluation of their choices over multiple criteria. More information, without reducing information processing costs, often leads to poor decisions under overload, and creates winner-take-all markets.

In most cultures people do not reveal their salaries and their general economic status even to their close friends and relatives. It is considered rude to reveal how much money you make and how wealthy you are, because any revelation leads to competition and one-upmanship. Ostentatious spending is frowned upon, and acceptable spending is defined by the spending habits of your peer group. The size of your house for example has little to do with your space needs, but has much more to do with the size of your friends' and neighbors' houses and how you compete with them. Any increase in the size of your house prompts everybody else to increase the size of their houses also, to make sure they still belong to the same identification group. The average size of a residential home has nearly doubled in the US during the last 50 years, while the average family size declined by 15% [31]. There is a cascading effect of imitation all along the social spectrum, because people would like to change their identification group to those that are slightly better than themselves, and hence influenced by the lifestyles of those slightly better off than themselves. Consequently, the super-wealthy influence the wealthy, who influence the upper middle class, who influence the masses. People constantly enlarge their notion of "what kind of a house does a person like me live in." One can trace this change in perception of what is normal, to increasing availability of information about other people's lifestyles both in the mass media and also in the social media. Information encourages competition; lack of it suppresses it.

The whipping effect of information on competition is wonderfully demonstrated by the fictional story "Christmas is Giving" by Malcolm Gladwell, in which two neighbors get into an unending competition of Christmas giving, trying to outdo each other. Every time they find out about a good deed done by the other, each one feels obligated to match it or even outdo it. Before long, they are giving away their furniture and appliances. The story ends when they run out of things to donate, after donating their home to the homeless, their organs to the sick, and their children to pedophiles [107]! Christmas giving by real people is not terribly different, and it is influenced heavily by other people's behavior. Everybody is anxious about doing what is expected by their community, and not falling behind. That is why churches and charitable organizations often issue guidelines to the community as to how much giving is expected on Christmas and what the community standards are.

On the other hand, those who are trying to claim superiority over others, and the elites who are trying to distinguish themselves from the masses, try to advertise their wealth through ostentatious spending, which spurs a cascading effect, and leads to increasing competition. That is whole reason of course why people buy bigger houses in the first place, to prove that they are different from the masses. That is why people buy expensive cars, and designer clothes. After all, the only way you can prove that you are part of the elite is by doing things that the masses cannot do; and that is the only way you can join the elite activities, attract elite mates, and make elite connections. There is evidence that this is the reason why fashions, baby names, and even accents change over time. Elites are always trying to distinguish themselves from the masses by wearing different clothes, using creative names, and changing the way they speak. Masses are constantly trying to imitate them as best as they can to be included in the privileged classes. That leads to an ongoing and unending change and competition. Social standards and restrictions try to limit such vicious cycles [58].

The impact of other people's wealth on one's wellbeing is not just psychological. Wealth is all relative, and other people's wealth directly impacts your economic wellbeing. So, it is not surprising that wide availability of information about wealth spurs a competitive reaction. We are all competing for the same goods that we need for our survival and our wellbeing. If others are wealthier, they will push the prices up, and lead to a decline in our real wealth and wellbeing. More importantly, modern societies are characterized by economic interdependence. We are all specialized and we all need the services of others for our basic necessities. So, our wealth is defined not just by what we own, but also how much we have to pay others for their services. If others are wealthy, their willingness to work for low pay diminishes, and that directly reduces our wealth. That is why people in India or South Africa feel wealthier than people in the US or Europe, even when their income is at the same level. It is because they have large numbers of very low-income people willing to work for very low wages, and their services are available to others at a very low price. That is why there is strong resistance to minimum wage laws in the US, even by some lower income people, because having some people at a lower income than yourself makes you better off economically by relying on the cheap services of those people.

Governments are information rich institutions since they are virtual constructs created to enable large-scale cooperation. But how much information is revealed about the government determines the amount of competition required for those coveted government positions. In the resource-rich environments of wealthy nations and at peace time, increasing competition is affordable and encouraged. Democracies emerge in this environment where lots of information have to be processed by the masses to elect the representative governments. In the resource-poor environments or at war time, such internal competition cannot be afforded, so the governments tend to be more authoritarian. They limit what information is revealed to the public, and what the public can discuss and debate, curtailing competition. Authoritarian regimes can be very efficient in the short run, because internal competition is costly and information intensive. There is the old adage of how "Nazis made the trains run on time in Germany". They probably did, as they stifled political wrangling over infrastructure development, and moved forward with a national unity and urgency to improve life. Yet, in the long run, there is a price to be paid for the efficiency of authoritarian regimes, and that is the difficulty for the minorities and the powerless to be heard and to influence policy, leading to increasing disgruntlement and instability. The powerless in authoritarian societies often have no recourse but to rebel and resort to violence to be heard, either in the form of crime, or in the form of civil war. Democracies on the other hand are inefficient and overly competitive, but more stable in the long-run, because they allow civil dissent. There is an optimum amount of competition in every society that can be achieved by limiting what information is available for the democratic process; but in an environment with free press, that limit is difficult to enforce, and the loudest and shrillest voices often dominate the democratic process. In 2015, the presidential election news is being dominated by Donald Trump, a real estate mogul with little political experience, because he is willing to make the most controversial statements that get him extensive publicity. More information is not always better in a highly competitive and intensely political environment. There is a need to effectively filter information for a democracy to function well. Mass media where all speak to all leads to an overload very quickly, and only the wealthiest and the most outrageous can get any attention. Modern social networks may be a useful remedy where information spreads through the trusted connections locally and custom-filtered, rather than through the large media empires designed for general consumption, or through the unfiltered public internet.

CHAPTER 12

SOLUTIONS

The primary reason for excessive competition is the mass communication technologies and the resulting mass markets that force all businesses and individuals into global competition. Electronic social networks create an opportunity to return to an earlier model of information dissemination, by propagating through networks, rather than direct broadcasting to the masses. There are four approaches to accomplishing this objective, in increasing level of sophistication:

a. Mass dissemination of information can simply be replaced with personalized dissemination through a network of trusted partners. This is similar to viral dissemination of popular videos and photos on social networks like Facebook. Each person is connected to its trusted partners, and the information travels by each person posting it to its partners. The popularity of viral videos and twitter feeds is a testament to the effectiveness of such a peer-to-peer propagation [29].

b. In a more sophisticated network, individuals can assign weights to their trusted partners, indicating the level of trust, so that they can further restrict the amount of information they receive, and better control the quality. They can limit their information intake to messages with a certain level of trust, computed by aggregating the trust levels of all the partners approving that message, and possibly by subtracting the trust levels of all those disapproving the message. Alternatively, all messages from trusted partners are received, but they are ranked and prioritized according to the total trust value attached to each.

A variation on this approach is to create a global trust value for each piece of information, product, or service, by aggregating the trust values attached to that piece by all raters, but also by weighting each trust value by the trustworthiness of the rater. The trustworthiness of the rater is also established in the same fashion recursively, by aggregating all the trust values it received, themselves weighted by the trustworthiness of the raters. Such recursive definitions are common in Computer Science, and Google's Web Search Engine works like this. Google's famous Page Rank search algorithm uses links incoming to a webpage as votes of trust, and simply counts them to calculate the total trust on that page, but it also weights each link according to the trustworthiness of its source, recursively defined in the same manner, by counting its incoming links, and weighting hem according to their source, ad infinatum [18].

This method has considerable potential in evaluating the trustworthiness of all information ranging from movie and restaurant recommendations, to judging the quality of academic papers or finding a reliable doctor. Such peer-to-peer evaluation maybe most effective in judging the quality of professional services, and the electronic social networks can accomplish this efficiently in very large scale. The evaluation of academic articles for example can be accomplished without an infrastructure of journals, editors, publishers, and reviewers. Articles can be self-published into digital repositories, and rated by all readers. Then an evaluation scheme, similar to Google's Page Rank, can easily aggregate all those ratings, weighted by the trustworthiness and the professional standing of those raters. The trustworthiness of the reviewers is similarly computed by aggregating the ratings they received, themselves weighted by the trustworthiness of the raters. Such recursive definitions have proven to be very effective in Search Engines. Furthermore, incentives can be devised to encourage more reviews and to improve the quality of reviews, by linking the trustworthiness of reviewers to the quality and the quantity of the reviews they submit, and the quality of the reviews themselves are determined recursively by the ratings they receive weighted by the trustworthiness of the raters. In effect, everything is rated recursively by everything else. Such a system can greatly reduce the cost, and increase the speed of academic publishing, and significantly improve the quality of reviews by aggregating them over larger samples than currently possible [Davis]. Current recommendation systems are based on a faulty assumption that all recommendations and ratings are equally valuable, and they are rated equally in computing aggregate ratings. When in fact, raters and recommenders are vastly different both in terms of qualifications and experience, and also relevance to specific individuals. Some systems attempt to limit the ratings to only those individuals who might be similar demographically, or might have engaged in specific transactions that make them more relevant, as in Amazon's "those who bought this also bought that", or Spotify's "those who are similar to you liked this music" type of systems. But these attempts are in their infancy, and they fail to assign varying weights to recommendations based on multiple factors of competence, reliability and relevance to a particular individual consumer.

c. The next level of sophistication and complexity involves complete delegation of some decisions to trusted partners. Once you establish the trustworthiness of an agent from their previous interactions with you, or with your trusted partners, or transitively with their trusted partners, following the network connections to arbitrary depth, then you can safely delegate some decisions to trustworthy agents. This is where both economic and political decision making can be drastically altered and improved. The approach would be similar to delegating medical decisions to your doctor, or legal decisions to your lawyer, since clearly they have specialized knowledge and they are better equipped to make decisions on your behalf than you could; and you have established trust with them through a mechanism of professional certification, recommendations from others you trust, and your own past experiences with them. This informal process of establishing trust can be replaced with a more formal and elaborate system relying on electronic social networks, where you can aggregate recommendations and ratings from a much larger set of trusted partners and their trusted partners, and you can weight them according to the reliability of the source, and delegate only if the aggregate trust level exceeds a predetermined threshold. All professional credentials received, all accolades and reprimands conferred by professional organizations, and all evaluations and ratings by peers, are automatically included since they are all trusted agents in the system. All agents have incentives to provide correct ratings and evaluations, since their own trustworthiness depends on the quality of the ratings and recommendations they provided in the past. Incentives can be expanded by devising payment systems to remunerate trusted partners for their services in proportion to the utilization of their ratings and recommendations, and the utilization itself depends on the quality and the quantity of services they provided in the past [72].

d. Delegation does not have to be full. One could delegate decisions partially, or to a set of agents collectively. Partial delegation can be accomplished by delegating each agent a part of a decision, or delegating a decision to different agents under different conditions. For example, a medical decision can be delegated to one doctor if the illness is terminal and end of life decisions have to be made, and to another doctor if the illness is not life threatening; or the surgical and pharmaceutical parts of a treatment decision can be delegated to different doctors. Collective delegation can be accomplished by delegating a medical decision to a group of medical doctors, but only if they can reach a consensus, or follow the majority opinion [72].

Imagine electronic communities where consumption decisions are made collectively, as a result of some political process. For example, all community members purchase an item if a consensus is reached, or none does. This involves delegation of an otherwise individual consumption decision to the group. Some group purchasing communities like Groupon have such features. Imagine a public taxation system where individuals can direct their taxes partially or fully to specific government projects they trust; or direct their votes to trusted partners who in turn can direct their taxes to specific government projects for them, or vote for specific political candidates for them. This can be accomplished by joining a variety of electronic communities and allocating some of your taxes to those communities, then the community can vote collectively on various public issues or fund various government projects on behalf of its members. Communities may reach decisions through internal deliberations, or they may delegate their votes to a community leader for a period of time, who may in turn makes economic, political, and social decisions for the whole group. Such delegation may create considerable political power since the leader is empowered to speak for the whole group.

Such a system of delegation is considerably different from the current representative democracies where the power is also delegated to elected representatives, because under this system the delegation of power can involve many communities, each trusted in a very narrow context. That can lead to a more enlightened political process, since the community leaders can develop expertise and become quite knowledgeable in a very narrow context, yet wield considerable power in representing a large community in that narrow context. That would be similar to what lobbyists, local community leaders, and influential journalists do now informally; but can be formalized with actual delegated power, and developed in a much larger scale over electronic social networks. They can also be extended to multiple levels of delegation ranging from local communities like school boards, to national communities like labor unions, to even international communities like human rights groups, depending on the scope of the issue at hand. Such multi-level structures can be organized hierarchically to accommodate increasingly narrow contexts, and for consistent delegation and aggregation of power in those contexts. Such multi-level and narrowly targeted delegation systems have the potential to drastically change currently existing political systems, for two reasons. First, they convert an existing one or two level representative hierarchy into a multi-level hierarchy; and second, they convert the existing comprehensive delegation systems where political power is not dependent on context or issue, to a partial delegation system where each leader's delegated power is context-specific. For example, a representative may be able to vote on your behalf only on foreign policy issues, and another may represent your interests only on domestic infrastructure decisions, and each leader may represent varying numbers of people ranging from a handful to millions depending on the community structure and determined through a hierarchy of trust levels. Such flexibility in representation would lead to a distributed democracy with widely diffused power, and it would lead to distributed decision making at multiple levels of granularity while keeping them consistent through partial delegation [72].

CONCLUSIONS

Information is a powerful and dangerous product. It is not benign, neutral, or universally useful, as commonly assumed. Encouraging and maximizing information generation and novelty, at the expense of tradition and stability, may lead to unstable societies with no learning from the past. Efficient mass distribution of information may be the primary culprit in encouraging the production of large quantities of low quality information, and providing incentives to manipulate it and distort it, simply because of the emphasis on cheaper distribution rather than the more expensive quality production. There is a need to limit quantity and filter for quality. In earlier societies, tradition and culture acted as gatekeepers and limited what information is considered relevant and worthy of dissemination. The Amish in the US for example use the community elders as gatekeepers to filter information, and determine what information reaches the community. They block mass media and electronic communication, and filter out some technologies and some educational material on the basis of community interest. A similar institutional mechanism can be designed to build virtual communities that deliberately and carefully limit their information intake. That can be done by building centralized institutions that control information flow, as it was done successfully by the editorial staff of newspapers and television stations during the last century, but lost their effectiveness with the proliferation of distribution channels. It can also be done by relying on social networks where individuals can build their communities from the ground up and rely on that decentralized structure for filtering information. Uncontrolled mass distribution of information to all, and then expecting the individuals to sort out the quality for themselves, as it is encouraged by the cable television and internet technologies, appears to be a faulty model that encourages distortion and manipulation. It also creates a race to capitalize on short term advantages from information at the expense of others, with no long term cooperative planning.

Community standards and principles that can guide the generation and dissemination of information can go a long way to curb the information glut. World-wide institutions may also be necessary to prevent an emphasis on short term benefits from information, as in weapons systems, environmental pollution, and government and business propaganda. National and local institutions may supplant the global ones to act as trusted third parties to vet and filter locally relevant information. Finally, personal filters based on social networks may complete the multilevel system to reduce the harmful effects of low quality information. The design of such information delivery systems is a drastic departure from the current approach of maximizing information production and dissemination, with the prevailing assumption that more information is always better.

Information content of a society determines the social problems it faces. Previous changes in the information repository of humans created fundamental social problems. The knowledge of agriculture replaced hunter-gatherer societies with geographically-fixed communities with permanent borders. That allowed the exploitation of others' labor, and created permanent social classes because people could not easily leave their physical location. The knowledge of industrialization replaced blood-based communities with work-based communities. That created merit-based societies with conditional acceptance, and rejection of those who could not perform, leading to work as the basis of identity and personal value, and a decreasing emphasis on family and child rearing. It created the constant risk of losing one's community identification when one cannot perform adequately, leading to loneliness, depression, and anxiety related illnesses. Digital economy is replacing work-based communities with interest and lifestyle based virtual communities connected by communication technologies. That leads to individual as the social and economic unit with memberships in many ephemeral communities. This is likely to be the age of pretense and opportunism with no sense of permanence and enduring relationships. Individuals are likely to assume many identities with different personalities during their lifetime, and even simultaneously. These fractured personalities are likely to lead to a crisis of trust and reliability, and consequently a plethora of cognitive illnesses such as attention deficit disorder, paranoia, and schizophrenia. The solutions require enhancing virtual communities with physical qualities such as economic cooperation, sharing resources such as housing, food, and sex, cooperative child rearing, and joint vacations. Enforcing community principles and lifestyles may be able to create a sense of identity and permanence that transcends the virtual world and spills over to the physical world [4, 35].

REFERENCES

1. Adam G. Flying or Driving: Which is Safer? Science August 25 2010.
2. Adas M. *Machines as the Measure of Men: Science, Technology, and the Ideologies of Western Dominance.* Cornell University Press 1990.
3. Agresto J. The Suicide of the Liberal Arts. *The Wall Street Journal,* Aug 7 2015.
4. Alexander C. et al. *A Pattern Language: Towns, Buildings, Construction.* Oxford University Press 1977.
5. Andrews E. Christian Missions and Colonial Empires Reconsidered. *Journal of Church & State* 51, 2010.
6. Arel D. Religion is Not the Problem in the Middle East. *Salon,* Oct 14 2014.
7. Ariely D. *Predictably Irrational: The Hidden Forces That Shape Our Decisions.* Harper 2010.
8. Barmash I. *The Manipulated Society: How Advertising, Public Relations, and Mass Media Influence Public Opinion, Taste, and Purchases.* Beard Books 2009.
9. Batie S., Mercuro N. *Alternative Institutional Structures: Evolution and Impact.* Routledge Publishing 2008.
10. Batthacharrjee Y. Paranormal Circumstances. *Discover Magazine* 2012.
11. BBC. Iran Court Sentences Criminals to Buy and Read Books. http://www.bbc.com/news/blogs-news-from-elsewhere- 34200912 Sep 9 2015.
12. Beavers A.F. *Exploring Ancient World Cultures.* Evansville Press 1997.
13. Butz A. R. *The Hoax of the Twentieth Century.* Thesis and Dissertation Press 2013.
14. Cashmore E. *Celebrity Culture.* Routledge Books 2006.
15. Cassidy M. What is the Point of College? College Calculus. *The New Yorker* Sep 7 2015.
16. Chang H. J. *Bad Samaritans: The Guilty Secrets of Rich Nations.* Random House Books 2007.
17. Churchill W. An American Holocaust: The Structure of Denial. *Socialism and Democracy* 2013.
18. Davis H. *Search Engine Optimization.* O'Reilly Media 2006.
19. Dawkins R. *The Magic of Reality: How We Know What's Really*

True. Free Press 2011.

20. Diamond J. Guns, Germs, and Steel: The Fates of Human Societies. Norton Publishing 1990.
21. Easley D., Kleinberg J. *Networks, Crowds and Markets: Reasoning About a Highly Connected World.* Cambridge University Press 2010.
22. *The Economist.* The Lemons Problem. June 2011.
23. *The Economist.* Virtual Economies. Jan 2005.
24. Eliot T. S. Two Choruses from the Rock. In *The Waste Land and Other Poems.* Hartcourt Brace 1960.
25. Ellul J. *The Technological Society.* Vintage Books 1967.
26. Enns J. Editorial. *Journal of Experimental Psychology* 38,1, 2012
27. Ewald P.W. *Evolution of Infectious Disease.* Oxford Press 1996.
28. Farrell W. *Why Men Are the Way They Are.* Mc Graw Hill 1990.
29. Ford M. The Lights in the Tunnel: Automation, Accelerating Technology and the Economy of the Future. Create Space Publishing 2009.
30. Foucault M. *Discipline and Punish: The Birth of the Prison.* Random House 1975.
31. Frank R.H. *Luxury Fever: Money and Happiness in an Era of Excess.* Princeton University Press 2000.
32. Furubotn E., Richter R. *Institutions and Economic Theory: The Contribution of the New Institutional Economics.* University of Michigan Press 2005.
33. Galbraith J.K. Economics and the Public Purpose. Houghton Mifflin 1973.
34. Greco T. *The End of Money and the Future of Civilization.* Chelsea Green Publishing 2009.
35. Greenfeld L. *Mind, Modernity, Madness: The Impact of Culture on Human Experience.* Harvard University Press 2013.
36. Greenfield J. *Fund-Raising: Evaluating and Managing the Fund Development Process.* Wiley 1999.
37. Good P.I. Hardin J.W. *Common Errors in Statistics.* Wiley 2011.
38. Halperin, R. *Economies Across Cultures: Towards a Comparative Science of the Economy.* St. Martin's Press 1988.
39. Harari Y.N. *Sapiens.* Harper Collins 2015.
40. Harari Y.N. Why Humans Run the World. http://ideas.ted.com/why-humans-run-the-world/ ,2015.

41. Hedges C. War is a Force that Gives us Meaning. Anchor Publishing 2003.
42. Hess A. Let Them Blog: The Panic Over Pro-Anorexia Blogs. *Slate*, July 14 2015.
43. Hoffman A. *How Culture Shapes the Climate Debate*. Stanford University Press 2015.
44. Holmes J. The case for teaching Ignorance. *NY Times*, Aug 24 2015.
45. Jacobs T. The Unique Danger of Implied Misinformation. *Pacific Standard*, Sep 1 2015.
46. Jacobson N. Escape from Alienation: The challenge to Nation-State. *Representation* 84, 2004.
47. Jasanoff S. *States of Knowledge: The Co-production of Science and Social Order*. Routledge 2004.
48. Jeffcote R. Technology and Utopia. *Journal of Interdisciplinary and Cross-Cultural Studies* 3, 2003.
49. Jha S. When a bad surgeon is the one you want: ProPublica introduces a paradox. KevinMD.com July 23 2015.
50. Joseph S. What Doesn't Kill Us: The New Psychology of Posttraumatic Growth. Basic Books 2013.
51. Kahneman D., Slovic P., Tversky A. *Judgment under Uncertainty: Heuristics and Biases. Cambridge* 1982.
52. Kelly K. What Technology Wants. Penguin Books 2011.
53. Ketterer S. The Wage Gap Myth That Won't Die. *The Wall Street Journal*, Sep 30 2015.
54. Kipnis L. Sexual Paranoia Strikes Academe. *Chronicle of Higher Education*. Feb 15 2015.
55. Knight J. Sened I. *Explaining Social Institutions*. University of Michigan Press 1998.
56. Krugman P. *The Return of Depression Economics and the Crisis of 2008*. Norton 2009.
57. Levine J. *Harmful to Minors: The Perils of Protecting Children from Sex*. University of Minnesota Press 2002.
58. Levitt S. D. Dubner S. J. *Freakonomics: A Rogue Economist Explores the Hidden Side of Everything*. William Morrow 2009.
59. Loudin J. *The Hoax of Romance*. Prentice-Hall, 1981.
60. Manjoo F. Ad Blockers and the Nuisance at the Heart of the Modern Web. *NY Times,* Aug 19 2015.
61. McClintock E. A. Romantic Opportunities Appear to Influence Women's Sexual Identities. *Phys.org,* Aug 25 2015.

62. McGoey L. *An Introduction to the Sociology of Ignorance. Essays on the Limits of Knowing.* Routlage 2014.
63. McGovern J. Why Are We So Angry at the Other Side? http://ivn.us/2015/07/14/documentary-why-are-we-so-angry-at-the-other-side/,2015.
64. Miller M.C. Student Resorts to Prostitution to Meet NYU's Soaring Cost of Tuition. *Huffington Post*, Sep 9 2015.
65. Mitchell R. L. Ad Blockers: A Solution or a Problem. *Computer World*, Jan 15 2014.
66. Morozov E. *To Save Everything, Click Here: The Folly of Technological Solutionism.* Public Affairs Publishing 2013.
67. Mowshowitz A. Virtual Organization: Towards a Theory of Societal Transformation Stimulated by Information Technology. *Communications of the ACM* 4, 11, 2-3, 2003.
68. Murray K. How Doctors Die. *Nexus,* Nov 30 2011.
69. Newitz A. How Ashley Madison Hid Its Fembot Con From Users and Investigators. *Gizmodo,*   Sep 8 2015.
70. Novella S. Psychology Journal Bans Significance Testing. *Science Based Medicine,* Feb 25 2015.
71. Olds J. *The Lonely American: Drifting Apart in the Twenty-first Century.* Beacon Press 2009.
72. Orman L. The Design of Trust Networks. *Communications of AIS* 2015.
73. Orman L.V. *Technology and Its Discontents: The Deadly Embrace of Technology and Society.* Create Space Publishing 2013.
74. Orman L.V. Technology as Risk. *IEEE Technology and Society* 32, 2, 22-31, 2013.
75. Orman L.V. The Potential of Virtual Institutions. *IEEE Technology and Society* 30, 1, 56-64, 2011.
76. Park J. L. *Romantic Love is a Hoax: Emotional Programming to Fall in Love.* University of Minnesota Press 2014. http://www.tc.umn.edu/~parkx032/CY-HOAX.html
77. Pearl J. *Causality: Models, Reasoning, and Inference.* Cambridge University Press 2000.
78. Pinker S. *The Better Angels of Our Nature: Why Violence Has Declined.* Viking Press 2011.
79. Polanyi K. *The Great Transformation: The Political and Economic Origins of Our Time.* Beacon Press 2001.
80. Pratkanis A. R., Aronson E. Age of Propaganda: The Everyday

use and Abuse of Persuasion. W.H. Freeman 1992.
81. Reene J. *Stockholm Syndrome*. Betascript Publishing 2012.
82. Rosecrance R. *The Rise of the Virtual State: Wealth and Power in the Coming Century*. Basic Books 1999.
83. Rosen C. The New Meaning of Mobility. *The New Atlantis* 31, 40-46, 2011.
84. Rossland I. Why There Are No Taboos in Scandinavian Children's Books. *The Guardian*, Aug 25 2015.
85. Ryan C. Jetha C. *Sex at Dawn*. Harper Publishing 2011.
86. Sales N.J. Tinder and the Dawn of the Dating Apocalypse. Vanity Fair, Sep 2015.
87. Satran J. Whole Food Co-CEO's Admit to Overcharging Customers. *Huffington Post*, July 2 2015.
88. Schettler T. *The Toxic Sandbox: The Truth About Environmental Toxins and Our Children's Health*. Perigree Books 2007.
89. Slaughter S., Rhoades G. Academic Capitalism and the New Economy. Johns Hopkins University Press 2004.
90. Stivers R. *Technology as Magic: The Triumph of the Irrational*. Bloomsbury Academic 2001.
91. Storr W. *The Unpersuadables: Adventures with the Enemies of Science*. Overlook Press 2014.
92. Strauss V. The decline of Play in Preschoolers and the Rise of Sensory Issues. *The Washington Post,* Sep 1 2015.
93. Sullivan M. Awash in Data, Thirsting for Truth. *NY Times*, Sep 5 2015.
94. Tainter J. *The Collapse of Complex Societies*. Cambridge University Press 1990.
95. Taleb N. *The Black Swan: The Impact of the Highly Improbable*. Random House 2010.
96. Taubes G. Diet Advice That Ignores Hunger. *NY Times,* Aug 29 2015.
97. Tavris C., Aronson E. Mistakes Were Made, But Not by Me. Hartcourt Books 2007.
98. Tetlock P.E. Expert Political Judgment. How Good Is It? How can We Know? Princeton University Press 2006.
99. Thaler R. *MisBehavior*. Norton 2014.
100. Tracy J. *The Civil Disobedience Handbook: A Brief History and Practical Advice for the Politically Disenchanted*. Manic Press 2001.

101. Waits Tom. https://www.goodreads.com/author/quotes/101363.Tom_Waits

102. Welsh J. Scientists Who Found Gluten Sensitivity Evidence Have Now Shown It Doesn't Exist. *Business Insider*, Aug 19 2015.

103. Zerzan J. *Against Civilization.* Feral House 2005.

104. Zerzan J. *Twilight of the Machines*. Feral House 2008.

105. Zinn H. *A People's History of the United States.* Harper Publishing 2005.

106. Zuboff S. *The Support Economy: Why Corporations are Failing Individuals and the Next Episode of Capitalism.* Viking Books 2002.

107. Gladwell M. *What the Dog Saw and Other Adventures.* Little Brown 2009.

108. Sarnoff D. *Looking Ahead: The Papers of David Sarnoff.* McGraw Hill 1968.

109. Gladwell M. Thresholds of Violence. *The New Yorker*, Oct 19 2015.

110. Zimbardo P., Coulombo N. Man Disconnected: How Technology Sabotaged What It Is To Be a Male. Rider Publishing 2015.

111. Farrell W. The Myth of Male Power: Why Men Are the Disposable Sex. Simon&Shuster 1993.

112. Hayes C. *Twilight of the Elites.* Crown Publishing 2012.

113. Lasch C. *The Revolt of the Elites and the Betrayal of Democracy.* Norton Publishing 1995.

114. Ferdman R. A. Why People Think Total Nonsense is Really Deep. Washington Post, Dec 1 2015.

115. The Onion. The Gorilla Sales Skyrocket After latest Gorilla Attack. 49, 2, Jan 10 2013.

116. McNamee S. J., Miller R.K. Jr. *The Meritocracy Myth.* Rowman and Littlefield Pub 2014.

117. DeSchryver M., Spiro R.J. New Forms of Deep Learning on the Web. IGI Publishing 2010.